# Pretty Witty Cakes
BOOK OF
# SUGARCRAFT
## CHARACTERS

Quadrille
PUBLISHING

# Contents

**It is a pleasure to welcome you to my first cake-decorating book. I am thrilled to be sharing with you many of my top tips and techniques for creating sugar characters.**

When I began cake decorating, I could not find a book that provided full step-by-step tutorials for fondant characters. As a result, I developed my own methods – which I now use when teaching my students. In the past 3 years, I have taught thousands of students from 45 countries, both in my classes and online. It gives me so much joy to see a complete novice make a character from start to finish in just a short space of time, and I am always delighted to see photos of my online students' work. Those photos and the feedback I receive show me that my methods of teaching really work.

This book has been carefully designed so that, even if you are a complete beginner, you will be able to make the characters. I have insisted on step-by-step photographs that show you everything – just as I do in my videos and classes. I show you many of my tricks of the trade, which you can apply to any character, and I hope this will give you the confidence to create your own characters from scratch.

Those of you who are familiar with Pretty Witty Cakes will know that it was born in 2010, when I made a dramatic career change following the birth of my first child. They say that children change your life, but I could never have imagined that one day I would have my own cake-decorating book. My two boys – Barnaby, aged 5, and Bertie, aged 3 – are core to everything I now do with Pretty Witty Cakes. My business, the bright colours I use and the cheeky expressions, faces and mannerisms I give my characters, all come from observing my children every day. My aim with any character is to make it fun, interesting and a little bit 'witty', to inspire the playful side in adults and children alike.

Even if you are a beginner, creating characters doesn't need to take a great deal of time – especially if you are juggling cake-making with running a family or another job. My methods and techniques are simple, so you can achieve them quickly and easily. Everything I make starts as a ball, and all designs are based on simple shapes – ovals, sausages, and so on. If you can roll a ball, you can make any of my characters!

Throughout the book, I have included ideas for setting the characters on a cake. The book is intended as a detailed guide to modelling sugarcraft characters and complementary elements of decoration, and I have used every available space to demonstrate these techniques. I therefore do not include cake recipes, although I have given the size and shape of the cake used next to each completed project.

I have tried to create a book which you will find fun, as well as an invaluable companion when creating sugarcraft characters. I always encourage beginners to copy my characters to the letter, then, when they are more confident, to use the ideas and methods they have learnt to make their own creations. Whichever characters you attempt, take your time to follow the step-by-steps carefully, and most of all have lots of fun making *and* eating them!

# Tips and techniques

## Pastes

### Fondant (sugar paste)
All the characters in this book are made using fondant. This is also commonly known as sugar paste. It is a very versatile paste, making it easy to create many types of characters. Fondant is readily available in stores selling cake supplies, or you can make your own – there are many fondant recipes on the internet.

### Pre-coloured fondant
I generally work with white fondant, which I colour myself using paste colours. You can see the various shades that can be achieved using paste colours on pages 10–11. However, for very dark colours, or those that require a lot of colouring, I tend to use pre-coloured pastes. This includes black, brown, red and blue.

### Florist paste (gum paste)
For detailing on characters – such as items which need to dry hard – I use florist paste. This is also commonly known as gum paste. Florist paste dries more quickly and much harder than fondant. It is perfect for ruffled skirts, like that worn by the ballerina fairy (see pages 66–71).

### Storing paste
When working with any fondant or florist paste, ensure that you keep it well wrapped to prevent it drying out. Break off the amount that you need, then wrap the remainder in a food-safe bag. This will prevent the air drying out the paste. If you are storing the fondant for a few weeks, place it in a plastic bag, then in a plastic airtight container. This will help to keep it soft.

## Storing completed characters

Unlike paste that hasn't been modelled, never store a completed character in a plastic bag or container. The plastic will cause your paste to sweat and go very soft. The character will then droop, lose its shape and become very sticky to touch. Fondant characters should always be stored in a cardboard cake box. If stored correctly in this way, they can be made up to 4 weeks in advance. Remember, the fondant will harden as it dries, so pick up the characters carefully so you don't snap off an arm or a leg!

## Preparing your paste

You may find that it is very difficult to model from straight fondant. This will depend on the climate and humidity you are working in. If you wish, you can convert your fondant into modelling paste by adding Gum Tragacanth, CMC or Tylose powder. Each of these products will make the fondant easier to model with and help it to dry more quickly. The amount you need will vary according to the warmth and humidity in the room, but it is usually about 1 teaspoon per 250 grammes of fondant. Kneed the powder into the fondant and allow to settle for 2 hours. You can then work with the fondant in the same way as you would have without the powder. Gum Tragacanth, CMC and Tylose powder all perform the same role but most people have a preference. I tend to prefer Gum Tragacanth. See descriptions of all three substances on the right and overleaf.

### Gum Tragacanth

Gum Tragacanth is derived from the sap of a plant which grows in the Middle East. The sap is drained from the root of the plant and then dried. This forms a powder which doesn't taste of anything, smells horrible but is ideal for thickening fondant. The powder is a light cream colour and is very fine – it's best to avoid breathing in too much as it can induce coughing as it enters the lungs.

### CMC

CMC stands for Carboxymethyl cellulose. In short, it is the chemical version of Gum Tragacanth and looks exactly the same. CMC tends to work a bit faster than Gum Tragacanth and is also slightly cheaper.

### Tylose powder

This is a brand name for CMC, and it is effectively the same thing. It works in exactly the same way.

## Colouring paste

To colour fondant or florist paste, always use paste food colouring. Liquid food colouring will change the consistency of the paste, so should be avoided. Get a small amount of paste colouring on the end of a cocktail stick and add it to the fondant or florist paste. Work it between your fingers until it is fully mixed. To make the colour darker, simply add more paste colouring.

## White vegetable fat

If you find that your fondant dries out, you can add a little white vegetable fat, such as Trex or Crisco, to resoften it. Apply the fat with your fingertip and work it through the fondant.

## Measuring by eye

When making characters, try not to rely too much on weights and measurements set in books. Instead, use your eye to judge the size of a ball, the amount of fondant needed or the depth of colour. Over time, you will create your own style based on your preferences for proportions and design.

## Dusting paste

If, after making a character, you find that the colour is too bright or looks flat, you can use edible dusts and tints to bring it to life. Always dust with dry powder and a dry brush. This technique is particularly useful for dusting blusher onto fairies' cheeks or for creating a multi-tone effect on fish scales or a turtle shell, for example.

## Securing parts together

In most cases, you can stick parts together using edible glue or water on the tip of a brush. However, for heavier pieces, or more delicate items such as fairy wings, it may be better to use royal icing. For internal support (for instance, when attaching a head to a body), I use spaghetti. This can be pushed inside the character to form a spine. Avoid putting inedible items such as cocktail sticks inside your characters.

## Painting on fondant

Painting on fondant is a great way to create a beautiful texture or pattern. There are several ways to make edible paint. My preferred method is to mix a tiny amount of paste food colouring (on the end of a cocktail stick) with about 1 teaspoon of cooled boiled water. The more water you add, the more transparent the colour will be. To deepen the colour, add a little more colour paste. Another method I use is to mix about half a teaspoon of edible tint or lustre dust with half a teaspoon of dipping solution, lemon extract or vodka. The more tint you add, the thicker the colour will be. Vodka will dry more slowly than dipping solution or lemon extract due to a higher water content.

# Fondant colours

Many of the paste colour pots on the market today look black from the outside, so it's hard to tell what the colour will look like when added to fondant or florist paste. Here, I've set out 168 samples to demonstrate how the colours will appear in practice.

| | | |
|---|---|---|
| 1 RS white | 57 PME sunny yellow | 113 RS Atlantic blue |
| 2 SF super white | 58 SF daffodil pastel | 114 AM electric blue |
| 3 AM bright white | 59 AM electric yellow | 115 AM sky blue |
| 4 RS shell pink | 60 SF primrose | 116 SF navy |
| 5 SF liquorice | 61 SF daffodil pastel | 117 SF baby blue |
| 6 PME midnight black | 62 PME sunny yellow | 118 AM navy |
| 7 SF shadow grey | 63 RS white chocolate | 119 AM royal blue |
| 8 SF shadow grey | 64 SF cream | 120 RS navy |
| 9 SF black extra | 65 PME lime crush | 121 SF deep purple |
| 10 AM super black | 66 SF lemon/lime | 122 AM regal purple |
| 11 SF liquorice | 67 SF lemon/lime | 123 SF grape violet |
| 12 SF eucalyptus | 68 AM electric green | 124 PME regal purple |
| 13 RS grey | 69 PME lime crush | 125 RS amethyst |
| 14 RS bottle green | 70 SF mint green | 126 AM electric purple |
| 15 PME midnight black | 71 SF spring green pastel | 127 AM fuchsia |
| 16 AM super black | 72 AM mint green | 128 AM electric purple |
| 17 SF black extra | 73 SF spring green pastel | 129 SF lavender pastel |
| 18 RS black | 74 SF party green | 130 SF grape violet |
| 19 RS chocolate brown | 75 SF Christmas green | 131 SF deep purple |
| 20 AM chocolate brown | 76 RS pastel green | 132 PME regal purple |
| 21 SF dark brown | 77 SF spruce green | 133 AM regal purple |
| 22 SF dark brown | 78 SF peppermint pastel | 134 RS lilac |
| 23 SF ivory/caramel | 79 SF holly green | 135 SF lavender pastel |
| 24 RS teddy bear brown | 80 AM avocado | 136 SF dusky pink |
| 25 AM chocolate brown | 81 SF eucalyptus | 137 AM fuchsia |
| 26 SF brown pastel | 82 SF gooseberry | 138 SF pink |
| 27 AM ivory | 83 RS lime green | 139 SF baby pink pastel |
| 28 SF autumn leaf | 84 SF gooseberry | 140 PME hot pink |
| 29 AM gold | 85 AM avocado | 141 RS baby pink |
| 30 SF egyptian orange | 86 SF holly green | 142 SF claret |
| 31 SF ivory | 87 SF spruce green | 143 SF burgundy |
| 32 SF autumn leaf | 88 SF Christmas green | 144 PME berry red |
| 33 AM ivory | 89 RS Lincoln green | 145 SF poppy red |
| 34 AM gold | 90 AM electric green | 146 SF ruby |
| 35 SF brown pastel | 91 SF mint green | 147 SF red extra |
| 36 RS flesh | 92 AM mint green | 148 AM soft pink |
| 37 PME tiger lily | 93 SF party green | 149 SF baby pink pastel |
| 38 SF flesh/paprika | 94 SF peppermint pastel | 150 AM super red |
| 39 SF orange pastel | 95 AM teal | 151 AM electric pink |
| 40 SF tangerine/apricot | 96 RS jade green | 152 SF scarlet pastel |
| 41 SF orange pastel | 97 SF turquoise | 153 PME hot pink |
| 42 PME tiger lily | 98 SF sky blue pastel | 154 AM electric pink |
| 43 SF flesh/paprika | 99 RS duck egg blue | 155 AM soft pink |
| 44 SF tangerine/apricot | 100 SF navy | 156 SF scarlet pastel |
| 45 AM electric orange | 101 SF baby blue pastel | 157 SF pink |
| 46 RS orange | 102 AM navy | 158 RS fuchsia |
| 47 SF egg yellow | 103 AM royal blue | 159 PME berry red |
| 48 AM electric orange | 104 RS baby blue | 160 SF ruby |
| 49 SF egg yellow | 105 AM teal | 161 SF red extra |
| 50 SF egyptian orange | 106 SF ice blue | 162 RS poppy red |
| 51 SF cream | 107 AM sky blue | 163 AM super red |
| 52 RS yellow | 108 AM electric blue | 164 SF poppy red |
| 53 SF melon | 109 SF sky blue pastel | 165 SF claret |
| 54 SF primrose | 110 SF turquoise | 166 SF ruby red |
| 55 SF melon | 111 RS turquoise | 167 SF burgundy |
| 56 AM electric yellow | 112 SF ice blue | 168 SF dusky pink |

**KEY**
**SF** Sugarflair
**AM** Americolor
**RS** Renshaw Sugarpaste
**PME** PME

Please note: Some colours are listed twice, to show the effect when you use both a tiny amount of paste and a greater amount.

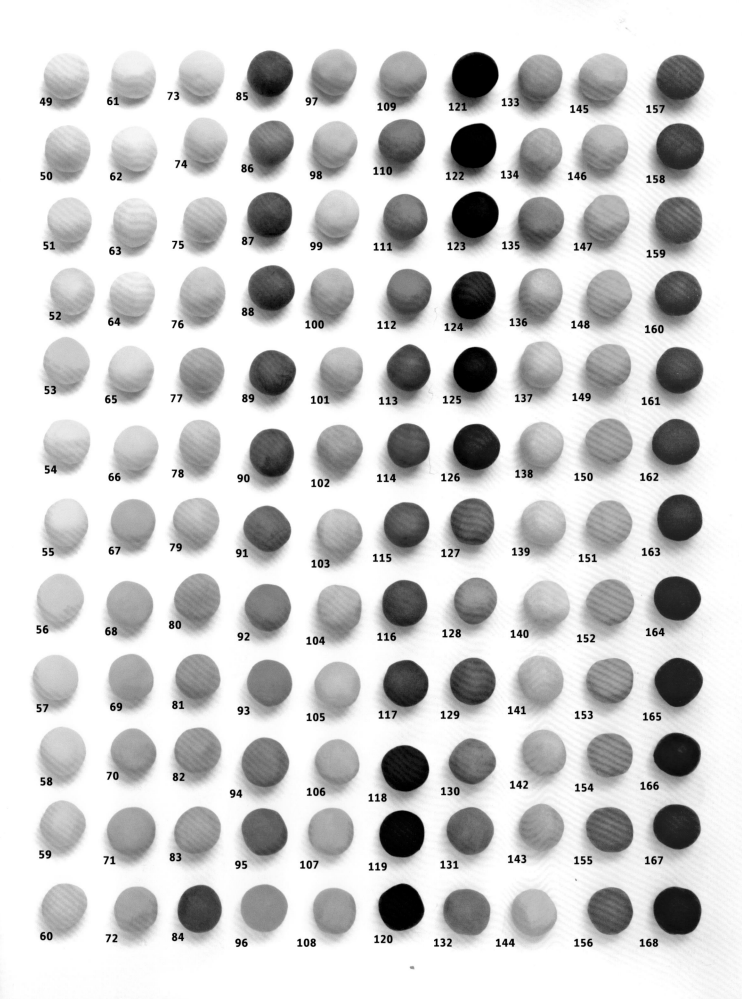

# Basic modelling kit

Your number one tool when modelling fondant characters is your hands. Almost everything in this book can be made using your fingertips, along with a few key tools. Not all of the items listed below are used in every project, but for regular sugarcrafters this is all useful equipment. It is a good idea to look through the step-by-steps to see which of these items are required for a particular project before you get started.

1   Piping gel with Sugarflair ice blue paste colouring
2   Non-stick board
3   Edible glue
4   Scalpel
5   Size 1 sable brush
6   Size 2 sable brush
7   Size 3 sable brush
8   Dried spaghetti
9   Toothbrush
10  Petal veiner / friller tool
11  Foam flower tray
12  Foam flower pad
13  Craft gun
14  Hair nozzle for craft gun
15  Rope nozzle for craft gun
16  Wire cutters
17  Various piping nozzle shapes for patterning, including size 2, 10 and 103
18  Gum Tragacanth (or CMC or Tylose powder)
19  White vegetable fat (Trex or Crisco)
20  Oval cutters in various sizes

21  Edible tints
22  Edible colour pastes
23  Wedge colour shaper
24  Cup chisel colour shaper
25  Flat-ended colour shaper
26  Pointed colour shaper
27  Angle chisel colour shaper
28  Round cutters in various sizes
29  Black edible ink pen
30  Metal ruler (with measurements to the edge)
31  Non-stick rolling pin
32  Crafted palette knife
33  Smile tool
34  Wheel tool
35  Ball tool
36  Pin tool
37  Stitching / quilting tool
38  Cocktail sticks
39  Tear / rose petal cutters in various sizes
40  Dipping solution, lemon extract or vodka
41  Small pointed scissors

# Safari Animals

# Flumpy

## THE ELEPHANT

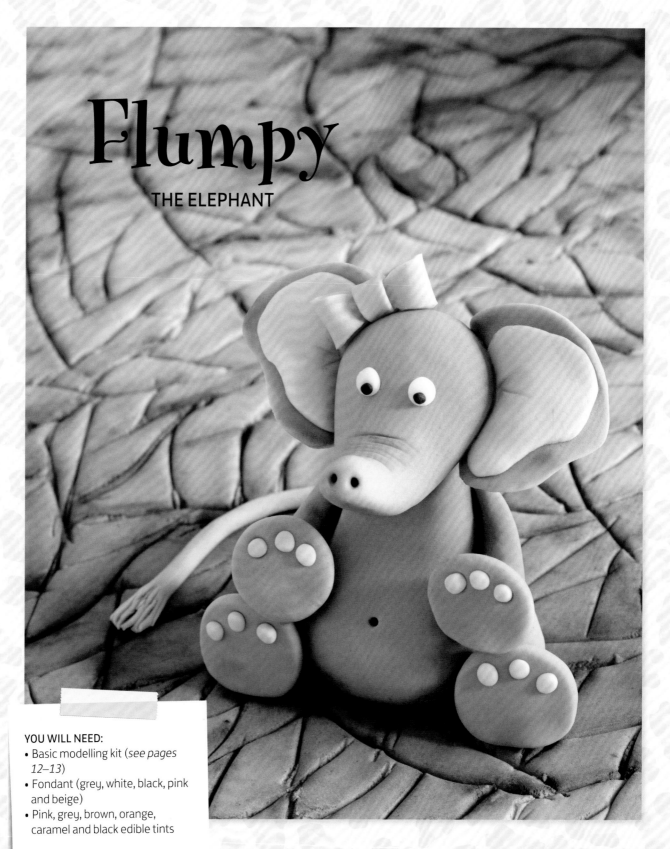

**YOU WILL NEED:**
- Basic modelling kit (*see pages 12–13*)
- Fondant (grey, white, black, pink and beige)
- Pink, grey, brown, orange, caramel and black edible tints

You can make this character any size you choose. For the size shown here, use the templates on page 180. The fondant colours for Flumpy are grey, white, black and pink. For the accessories you will need beige fondant.

1. Roll 6 balls of grey fondant: a body, a head, 2 arms and 2 legs.

2. Take the largest ball and roll into a cone shape.

3. Stand the cone with the small end pointing upwards. Using your thumb, push down on the front to make a curve and a fat tummy.

4. Compare the head ball with the body. The head ball should be about half the height of the body.

5. Place your index finger halfway across the head ball and gently rock it backwards and forwards to make the trunk.

6. Use the tip of your finger to soften the trunk. Make sure it isn't too long (about the same length as the top third of your finger).

7. Push a piece of spaghetti into the body, pushing it all the way to the bottom. Leave a small amount showing at the top. Place the head onto the body. Don't add glue at this stage.

8. Using a cocktail stick, poke 2 holes in the end of the trunk to make the nostrils.

9. Make 2 holes where you want the eyes to be and add glue with a small brush. Roll 2 equal-sized white fondant balls.

10. Push the balls against the glued holes. The fondant will sink into the holes a little.

11. Add tiny balls of black fondant to make the pupils, then attach to the eyes with edible glue.

Use the blunt side of a scalpel to make creases in the trunk.

Take the balls of fondant that you put aside for the legs and roll them into cone shapes.

Hold each cone between your thumb and index finger and tap on the table to create a flat foot.

Glue the legs to the sides of the elephant. The backs of the legs (the hip area) should be pushed flat against the elephant.

Use a small ball tool to make 3 indents in each foot.

Repeat steps 13–16 to make the arms. They should be slightly thinner than the legs, but a bit longer so they can rest on the feet. Glue them to the body.

Make indents in the base of the arms as in step 16. Roll 12 equal-sized pink balls, add a dab of glue to the 12 indents and push in the pink balls until flat.

Before moving forward, glue on the head. Next, roll out a piece of grey fondant on a non-stick board.

Cut out 2 pieces with a tear cutter. (Bigger ears make cuter elephants.)

Cut a piece from each side of both tear shapes as shown.

Cut off the points.

Using your finger, soften the outline to remove any jagged edges so the ears are nicely rounded.

24

Roll out some light pink fondant on a non-stick board. Cut out 2 shapes using the same cutter as in step 20.

25

Slice the edges off the pink pieces, making them smaller than the grey pieces and oval in shape.

26

Glue the pink pieces into the oval part of each ear, leaving the square edge clear.

27

Apply glue to the square edge.

28

Glue the ears to the sides of the elephant's head.

29

Make creases inside the ears using the back of a scalpel.

**TOP TIP**
When making an elephant, always position the ears around the side of the head. If you push them up to the top of the head, your elephant will turn into a mouse! Elephant ears can be as big as you wish and will give character to your design.

30

Using the same grey fondant, roll a sausage shape for the tail, making one end more bulbous than the other.

31

Using a scalpel, cut lots of slits in the bulbous end. Glue the tail to the back of the elephant.

32

Roll out a small piece of pink fondant and cut a long strip. Put a dab of glue in the middle.

33

Fold the ends into the middle, leaving loops to form a bow. Cut a smaller strip of fondant and place over the join, gluing into position.

34

Use a scalpel to trim the ends so they are flush with the edges of the bow. Tuck the ends underneath.

35

TOP TIP
When using dipping solution, be careful not to touch your cake after you have painted it because the dipping solution will not set the paint and you can smudge your pattern. If you are worried about smudging, use lemon extract instead because this sets a little more.

Glue the bow onto the elephant's head and dust the creases in the ears with dark pink edible tint for extra definition. You can also dust the creases on the trunk and around the legs with grey edible tint.

1     Savannah floor

2

3

Cover your cake board with light brown or beige fondant. Use a wheel tool to make a random jagged pattern.

Use a cocktail stick to scrape over the lines, to make them rough-edged.

Dust the surface with edible tints in browns, oranges and caramels. Fill the cracks with dark brown tint mixed with a few drops of dipping solution.

1

Animal-print pattern

2

Use edible tint in your chosen colours. Here, I've used black and pink. Mix with a few drops of dipping solution.

Paint pink patches onto the icing on your cake, and outline in black. Ensure the pattern is random and the black edges don't meet.

CAKE DESIGN
For the design shown opposite, I positioned the elephant on a cake approximately 12 cm in diameter and 15 cm in depth. I hand-painted the entire cake and board with the animal-print pattern. If you position your elephant on a cake as shown in this suggested design, make sure you glue her in place with edible glue or a little royal icing.

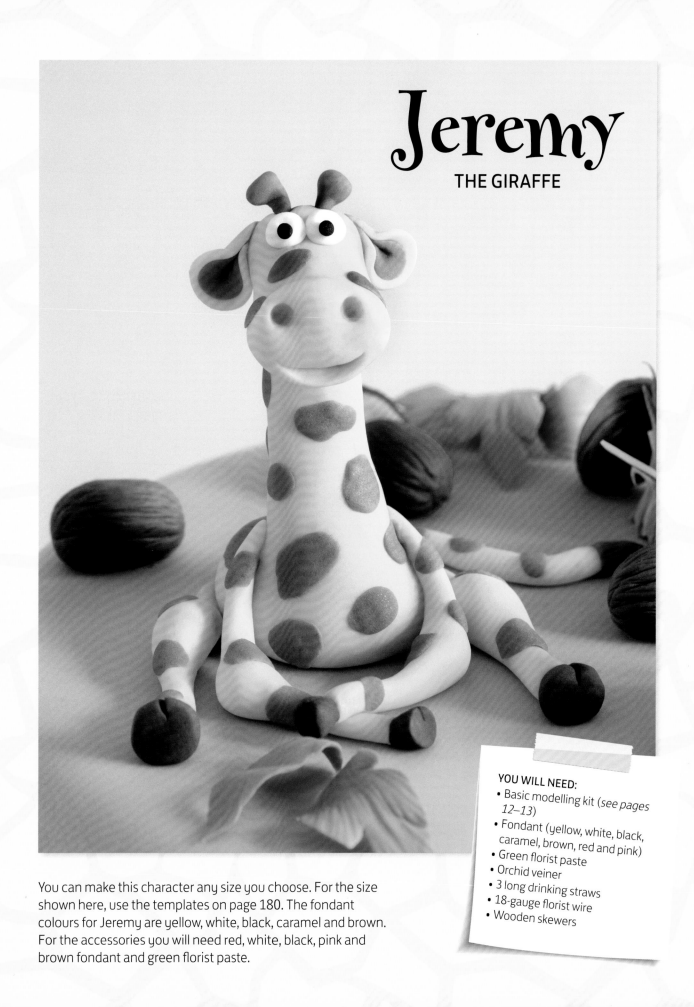

# Jeremy
## THE GIRAFFE

**YOU WILL NEED:**
- Basic modelling kit (*see pages 12–13*)
- Fondant (yellow, white, black, caramel, brown, red and pink)
- Green florist paste
- Orchid veiner
- 3 long drinking straws
- 18-gauge florist wire
- Wooden skewers

You can make this character any size you choose. For the size shown here, use the templates on page 180. The fondant colours for Jeremy are yellow, white, black, caramel and brown. For the accessories you will need red, white, black, pink and brown fondant and green florist paste.

Roll 2 balls of yellow fondant for the body and head.

Roll the larger ball into a cone but elongate the neck, making it as tall as you wish (about 8 cm is best).

Push a spaghetti stick (2 if needed) through the length of the fondant. For a cute giraffe, give him or her a big bottom!

Roll the smaller ball with your finger so there is a dip in the middle and the 'brain end' is smaller than the 'mouth end'.

Position the head on top of the long neck, inserting the spaghetti into the fondant (do not stick). Use a small ball tool to create 2 nostrils. To make the nostrils more flared, pinch the fondant between the ball tool and your finger.

Remove the head to add details to the face. To make a smile, gently push one side of a size 2 nozzle into the fondant.

Use a small ball tool to make indents for the eyes. With a cocktail stick, make 2 holes above the eyes for the brown giraffe knobs.

Roll 2 white balls (larger eyes are cuter than smaller ones) and glue them into the indents made in the previous step.

Roll 2 small balls of black fondant and glue them onto the eyes to make the pupils.

Make some brown fondant (add orange for a caramel tone) and roll 2 small balls.

Roll both balls into cones and pinch to create a little knob at the larger end.

**12**

Cut off the pointed end of each knob.

**13**

Put a dab of glue into the holes you made in step 7 and attach the knobs.

**14**

At this point, your giraffe should look like this.

**15**

Roll small balls of brown fondant and press flat on a non-stick board. Make the edges irregular.

**16**

Press the first brown patch onto the body. Use a flat-ended colour shaper to smooth down the edges so they merge with the yellow.

**17**

Repeat all over the body and head as desired.

**18**

For the ears, cut 2 yellow tear shapes using a cutter 1.5 cm long.

**19**

Cut 2 smaller brown tear shapes using a cutter about 1 cm long, then glue them to the yellow shapes. Ensure that they are closer to the edge at the rounded end.

**20**

Take 1 ear and fold over the pointed end, then curl in the edges.

**21**

Chop off the pointed end.

**22**

Repeat steps 20–21 to make the other ear, then attach both ears and point them downwards so they look floppy.

**23**

Using yellow fondant, roll 2 large balls, 2 medium-sized balls and 1 small ball.

**24**

To make a leg, roll 1 of the larger balls as shown. This will create a knee area and a sausage shape at each end.

Roll out the fondant until the leg is fairly long and thin, making sure the knee isn't too big.

Cut off one end to make a flat edge and pinch the other end between your thumb and finger.

TOP TIP
Fondant is very pliable. If you find it too stiff or it cracks, reduce the amount of Gum Tragacanth (or CMC or Tylose) you are using. You can model without the added powders once you are more confident.

To make a hoof, roll a small ball of dark brown fondant.

Roll into a cone shape, then tap the cone on your work surface to make a flat base.

Cut off the top of the cone and discard. Glue the remaining piece to the flat end of the leg to make a foot..

Cut a small groove in the front of the foot to create hooves.

Cover the leg in brown patches as you did with the head and body. Use the flat-ended colour shaper to smooth down the edges.

Make a second leg in the same way, but bending in the opposite direction.

Attach both legs to the base of the body using edible glue.

To make the arms, repeat steps 24–32 using the medium-sized balls. The arms should bend more sharply at the elbow.

Attach the arms at the shoulder and cross 1 arm over the other.

**Safari Animals**  **25**

36

For the tail, roll the smallest ball into a sausage shape and cut off one end. Bend the tail and flatten the other end with your fingertip.

37

To make the hair, roll a small ball of brown fondant into a cone shape and cut off the rounded end.

38

Cut off the flattened end of the tail. Glue the hair to the other end and make hair lines with a wheel tool. Add patches.

39

40

Attach the tail to the back of the giraffe with edible glue. Let him sit on it slightly. If you wish, you can rotate the giraffe's head as shown. Glue in place once you're happy with the overall position.

### Cecil the Snake

1

Roll a ball of red fondant into a long pointed sausage.

2

Bend the thinner end and raise the fatter end to stand upright.

3

Use the wide end of a size 2 nozzle to make a mouth, then make indents for the eyes using a pin tool.

Roll 2 small white balls for the eyes and glue in place. Use 2 tiny black balls for the pupils. Thinly roll out a strip of light pink fondant and cut out triangles.

Fix the triangles in place along the length of the snake using edible glue.

Your finished snake should look like this.

## Coconuts

Roll an oval of white fondant about 1 cm wide and 1.5 cm long, then place it on top of a rectangle of brown fondant.

Wrap the brown fondant around the oval and close 3 sides. Cut triangles in the open end, then seal. Roll in your hand to smooth out the joins.

To make the hair pattern, roll over the surface using a wheel tool.

Cut some of the coconuts in half and use a large ball tool to push in the white area.

Use the wheel tool to add texture to the cut side of the brown fondant.

## Leaves

Cut freehand large and small leaves from green florist paste.

Create veins using an embosser (here I have used an orchid veiner).

Leave to dry on a curved surface, such as a large non-stick rolling pin, for at least 2 hours and ideally 24 hours.

## Tree

Wrap 3 long drinking straws together with florist tape.

Push the straws into the cake, all the way to the bottom so they stand up.

Put 18-gauge florist wire into the straws and bend the tops to make branches. Fill the gaps with wooden skewers.

Using brown and light brown fondant, wrap strips around the trunk. Overlap them and secure with glue as you go up the trunk.

Cover the wires with brown fondant and glue a ball of fondant in the centre.

When the leaves are bone dry, glue 4 large leaves onto the fondant-covered wires.

Build up with more leaves by gluing them to the brown ball of fondant in the centre.

TOP TIP
All my characters are based on simple shapes. When I design any character, I build them as a series of circles, squares and rectangles. Working in this way, anyone can create an animal with human characteristics. Details can be added later.

CAKE DESIGN
The setting I've created here is just one example of how you can situate your giraffe. He will work well on any cake design or on a cupcake if made smaller. Here, I've used a round cake about 20 cm in diameter and 10 cm in depth. I've covered the cake with green fondant and placed the giraffe under the tree, surrounded by coconuts. You could insert the taped straws into a larger plastic dowel before covering in fondant. This will ensure your tree is totally food safe by preventing the wire or tape from coming into contact with the cake.

# Zachery
## THE ZEBRA

You can make this character any size you choose. For the size shown here, use the templates on page 181. The fondant colours for Zachery are white, grey, black and pink. For the accessories you will need red, yellow, mauve, green and blue fondant.

**YOU WILL NEED:**
- Basic modelling kit (*see pages 12–13*)
- Fondant (white, grey, black, pink, red, yellow, mauve, green and blue)
- Small heart plunger cutter
- Light muscovado sugar
- Teaspoon

1. Roll 2 white balls – 1 large and 1 small – for the body and head.

2. Roll the larger ball into a cone shape. Use your thumb to push down on the front to make a curve. Push a piece of spaghetti all the way to the bottom.

3. Place the smaller ball in your palm and roll one end so it becomes narrower than the other end.

4. Push the smaller ball onto the spaghetti. Do not glue.

5. Roll out some grey fondant to a depth of about 3 mm. Cut an oval shape about the same size as the wider end of the face.

6. Using your fingertips, squash the oval to make it thinner and larger.

7. Push the oval onto the end of the face and smooth down the edges to merge with the white.

8. Use a small ball tool to make 2 nostrils.

9. Using a size 2 nozzle, push one side of the large end into the fondant to make a smile (the more you push, the bigger the smile).

10. Use a cocktail stick or a pin tool to make 2 indents for the ears and 2 more for the eyes.

11. Roll 2 black balls to make the eyes and glue in place. Glue 2 tiny white balls on top, for pupils.

12. Roll 2 equal-sized balls for the ears. Taking each one in turn, pinch one end as shown, to form a triangle.

13. Cut off the rounded end of each piece. This will give you 2 soft-edged triangles.

14. Cut 2 small triangles of pink fondant and glue them to the larger white triangles.

15. Glue the ears into the grooves you made in step 10.

Roll out a piece of black fondant very thinly, then use a scalpel to cut out long triangles. Don't make them too perfect.

Position them all over the body in horizontal bands. They should be a little jagged.

Roll a few small balls of black fondant, then shape into long thin cones.

Cut the rounded ends off the cones and glue them between the ears.

Your zebra should now look like this.

For the legs, roll 2 white balls about 1.5 cm in diameter and roll out one end, leaving the other end ball-shaped.

Tap the ball end on your work surface to flatten the base of the foot.

Use a scalpel to cut a soft crease into the foot.

Place black fondant triangles on the legs, as you did with the body.

Roll out some black fondant and cut out 2 heart shapes using a small heart cutter. Glue them to the bases of the feet.

Glue the legs to the base of the body, tucking them underneath the body slightly.

Roll 2 white balls (about 1 cm in diameter) for the arms. Roll out one end.

Repeat steps 22–3 to make the arms, then attach heart shapes as in step 25.

Attach stripes and a small piece of black fondant to cover the join. Leave to dry for a few minutes.

**30**

While the arms are drying, roll a ball of white fondant and shape it into a tail. Cut off each end.

**31**

Roll a small ball of grey fondant and shape into a cone.

**32**

Attach stripes to the tail. Glue the flat end of the grey cone to one end of the tail, then mark lines on the grey piece with a wheel tool.

**33**

Attach the arms and the tail, ensuring the arms sit in front of the tail. Glue the head in place. (Always glue the pieces in place as late as possible, once you are happy with the zebra's position.)

**1** **Bucket**

Roll a cone of red fondant, then cut off the top and bottom.

**2**

Using a large ball tool, push the fondant against your finger to make a rim.

**3**

Wrap a thin strip of fondant around the rim of the bucket.

**4**

Cut a thin strip of yellow fondant and curve into an arch. Leave to dry for 1 hour.

**5**

Fill the bucket with light muscovado sugar (this resembles sand) and glue the handle in place.

**Spade**

**1**

Roll 2 sausages of yellow fondant – 1 long and 1 short – and glue together to form a 'T' shape. Roll an oval about 4 mm thick, then cut off one end.

**2**

Glue together, then use a large ball tool to shape the inside of the spade.

**1   Starfish**

On a non-stick board, roll out some mauve fondant to a thickness of 5 mm. Using a scalpel, cut out a freehand 5-pointed star.

**2**

Gently pinch each point between your thumb and finger to soften the edges.

**3**

Texture the surface using a small ball tool.

**4**

Make a smile with a nozzle. Glue on 2 white balls for eyes, with black pupils on top.

**Crocodile in the water**

**1**

Roll a green ball and cut off one side. Shape both pieces so they have flat bases and curved sides. Take the large piece and make indents for the eyes using a ball tool.

**2**

Fill the indents with 2 white balls, then add 2 tiny black balls to make pupils. The pupils should look up towards the zebra.

**3**

Add 2 small balls of green fondant to the top of the nose. Make indents with a small ball tool as shown.

**4**

Make a back shape (and, if desired, a tail) and pinch along the top to form a visible spine. Ensure this piece has a flat base.

**5**

Roll along the spine with a wheel tool. Insert small triangles of darker green fondant into the ridge. You can repeat this along the tail.

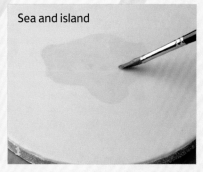

**Sea and island**

Cover your cake or board with light blue fondant, then paint edible glue over the area where the island will go.

Pour light muscovado sugar over the glue, building up an island. Pat down the sugar to compress. Remove any stray granules with a soft dry brush.

**3**

Put some piping gel in a bowl, then add a little ice blue paste food colouring and mix with a teaspoon.

**4**

Use the spoon to pour the blue piping gel onto the iced cake or board around the island, until all the blue fondant is covered.

TOP TIP
Piping gel is perfect for creating a water effect. If you find it too thick to pour from a spoon, heat in the microwave in 5-second bursts until it reaches the desired consistency.

CAKE DESIGN
You can set your zebra in the middle of a cake of any size. The piping gel can either sit flush with the top of the cake or you can leave a slight border.

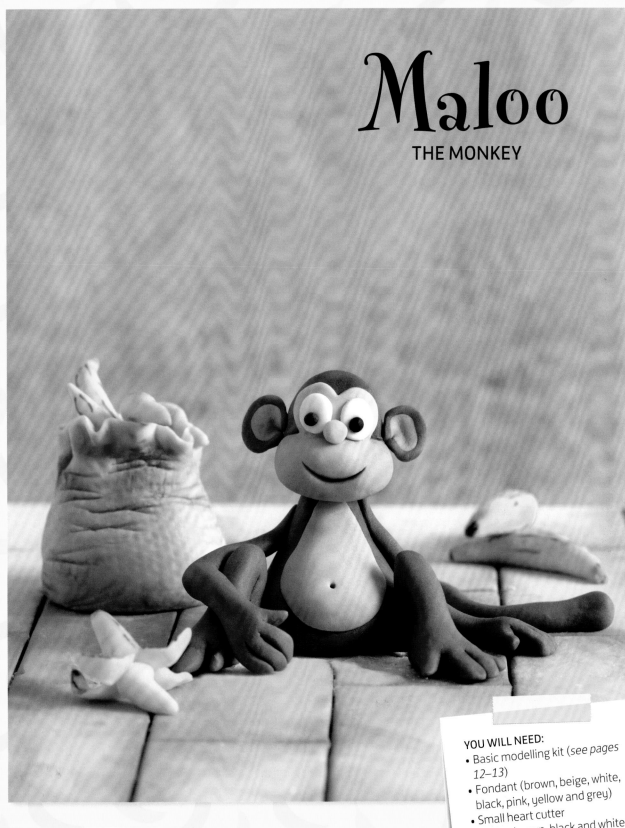

# Maloo
## THE MONKEY

You can make this character any size you choose. For the size shown here, use the templates on page 181. The fondant colours for Maloo are brown, beige, white, black and pink. For the accessories you will need yellow, white, beige, grey and brown fondant.

**YOU WILL NEED:**
- Basic modelling kit (*see pages 12–13*)
- Fondant (brown, beige, white, black, pink, yellow and grey)
- Small heart cutter
- Green, brown, black and white edible tint
- Black edible ink pen
- Fabric embossing mat
- Bark embossing mat

Roll 1 ball of brown fondant for the body and another for the top part of the head. Roll a beige ball for the lower part of the head.

Roll the largest ball into a cone shape. Using your thumb, press down in the middle to make a fat belly. Push a length of spaghetti through the body as shown.

Roll out some beige fondant and use a tear cutter to cut out a shape that fits onto the body.

TOP TIP
You can use the templates on page 181 to make your monkey exactly the same size as the one shown here, but if you judge the size by eye, you will start to know by instinct what size balls to use. In time, you will find that you start to make the balls the right size at the first attempt, without measuring.

Glue the tear shape to the tummy. Use a pin tool to make a belly button.

Take the medium-sized ball and flatten the top with the side of your thumb.

Place the small ball on top (you can apply glue, but this isn't essential).

Use the pointed colour shaper to blend the edges and create a seamless join. This piece will form the face.

Using a heart-shaped cutter, cut out one shape, then cut off the pointed end and discard.

Glue the remaing piece to the face as shown.

Use the pointed colour shaper to blend in the straight edge.

Make a smile by pressing the wide end of a size 2 nozzle into the face.

For the eyes, roll 2 equal-sized balls of white fondant and press flat.

Glue the eyes to the face and use a small ball tool to make indents for the pupils. Roll 2 tiny balls of black fondant and a small ball of pink fondant.

Glue the black balls into the indents made in the previous step, then glue the pink ball onto the centre of the face to make the nose.

Roll out some brown fondant and use a small tear cutter to cut out 2 shapes. Roll 2 small beige balls and flatten. Glue onto the tear shapes.

Take 1 piece and, using your finger and thumb, fold over the pointed end and pinch together. Then gently turn in the rounded end.

Cut off the pointed end. This completes 1 ear. Repeat steps 16–17 with the second piece.

Using the pointed colour shaper, make a hole in each side of the head for the ears to slot into.

Glue the ears into the slots.

Monkeys' ears tend to be perky rather than droopy.

Place the head on top of the body, pushing it onto the spaghetti support. You can glue the head in place now or wait until later.

For the legs, roll 2 brown balls and shape into long cones with a ball at one end.

Take 1 leg and bend in the middle to create a knee, then flatten the end opposite the ball (this will be tucked underneath the body).

**24** Gently press the ball-shaped end to create a foot.

**25** Using a scalpel, cut 1 big toe and 3 smaller toes (monkeys' feet look more like hands).

**26** Use your finger and thumb to round off the edges of the toes. Repeat steps 23–6 to make the other leg, making sure the big toe is on the other side of the foot.

**27** Glue the legs in place, tucking the end underneath the body.

**28** For the arms, roll 2 balls of brown fondant into long cone shapes (longer and thinner than the legs).

**29** Take 1 arm and bend in the middle, pinching to make an elbow.

**30** Flatten the wider end and gently bend. This will create a hand and forearm.

**31** As with the feet, cut 3 fingers and a thumb, but chop off the ends so the fingers aren't too long.

**32** Gently roll the fingers to soften the edges.

**33** Gently push the fingers and thumb together. Repeat steps 29–33 to make the second arm.

**34** Glue the arms in place at the shoulders. The paste will be soft enough for you to move the arms around until the position feels right.

**35** For the tail, roll a ball of brown fondant into a sausage shape. One end should be rounded. Bend the tail.

TOP TIP

If you want to make lots of animals that are all the same (for example for cupcakes) then make all bodies first, then all left legs and then all right legs and so on. You will work much faster as you repeat the same shape for each body, then each leg, each arm rather than make one whole animal followed by another.

Glue the thinner end of the tail in position at the back (let the monkey sit on it). At this point, check that you've glued all the limbs in place.

**Unpeeled bananas**

Mix some yellow fondant with white fondant to make a soft yellow ball.

Roll into a banana shape, with a soft point at each end.

Pinch the top to make a stalk, then use a scalpel to cut off the very end and create a flat edge.

Dust both ends with green edible tint.

Dust along the banana with brown edible tint.

Using black edible ink, draw lines along the banana and colour in the base.

## Peeled bananas

Using more of your soft yellow paste, roll a cone shape and cut off the wider end.

Slice the large end into quarters (cutting only halfway through the banana) and gently bend them outwards.

Pinch the 4 sections flat using your fingertips.

Dust the banana skin with brown edible tint, then use green edible tint to colour the base.

Add more white to your yellow fondant to make a very light yellow. Roll into a cone shape and glue into the banana skin.

Draw lines along the skin and colour in the base, using black edible ink. Your finished bananas should look like this.

## Sack

Roll a ball of beige or light brown fondant. Push in the top and pinch around the rim with your finger and thumb.

To create a gathered edge around the top of the sack, pinch hard all the way round using your thumb and finger (be careful not to break the fondant).

Use the back of a scalpel to create creases in the sides of the sack.

Add texture using a fabric embossing mat or a piece of fabric with a raised pattern.

Dust the creases with brown edible tint.

## Pavement

Cover a square cake board with grey fondant. Using a wheel tool, draw on the paving slabs (use a ruler if necessary).

Mix black edible tint with dipping solution, lemon extract or vodka to achieve paint consistency. Paint in between the slabs.

Using black, grey and white edible tint, dust the slabs to create shading. Make them darker nearer the painted lines and lighter in the middle.

### TOP TIP
When making accessories, add about 1 teaspoon of Gum Tragacanth, CMC or Tylose powder to 250 g of fondant to help it dry faster. This will make it easier to manipulate tiny details.

### Wood for the box

Roll out some brown fondant and cover with a bark embossing mat.

Put pressure on the mat to transfer the pattern to the fondant.

Cut the fondant into about 20 strips and attach a small ball of brown fondant to each end. Apply to your cake as shown opposite.

### CAKE DESIGN
In the picture opposite, I have used a sharp-edged cake (about 15 cm square and 10 cm in depth) to provide the box shape. I achieved this using 3 layers which I filled with ganache. I covered the cake in beige fondant and left it to dry for 24 hours until firm. I then placed the wood strips around the sides of the cake, letting the top strip sit 5 mm higher than the edge of the beige fondant. I left the wood strips to dry for a few hours before placing the cake on the pavement board. The board required at least 24 hours to dry and firm up. Finally, I added the monkey and bananas.

# ARIEL

## THE LION

You can make this character any size you choose. For the size shown here, use the templates on page 181. The fondant colours for Ariel are beige, brown, pink, white and black. For the accessories you will need florist paste in various shades of green.

**YOU WILL NEED:**
- Basic modelling kit (*see pages 12–13*)
- Fondant (beige, brown, pink, white and black)
- Soft pink and light brown edible tint
- Shades of green florist paste
- Leaf or orchid veiner
- Colour paste pots in shades of green

1

Roll 2 balls of beige fondant for the body and head.

2

Roll the larger ball into a cone shape.

3

Push a spaghetti stick vertically through the fondant, to create a support. Press the middle with your thumb to make a big round tummy.

4

Make a belly button using a pin tool or cocktail stick.

5

Roll the smaller ball into a cone shape.

6

Place the head on top of the body, pushing it onto the spaghetti. Don't glue it in position at this stage. Use your thumb to flatten the area where the eyes will go.

7

Roll 2 balls of beige fondant for the legs. Roll out 1 half of each ball to create a long cone shape, leaving a ball at the other end.

8

Take the first leg and pinch the ball-shaped end between your thumb and finger to make a flat foot.

9

Using a scalpel, cut 2 grooves in the foot to shape the paw.

10

Using a ball tool, make a small indent in the base of each toe and a large indent in the sole of the foot.

11

Roll 1 large brown ball and 3 smaller ones. Glue them into the indents and press the edges flat using a flat-ended colour shaper.

12

Repeat steps 8–11 to make the second leg. Glue both back legs in place at the base of the body.

**13**

Roll 2 balls of beige fondant for the arms. Roll out each piece to form a long sausage shape with a ball at one end.

**14**

Taking one arm, squash the ball slightly and pinch it upwards to form a front paw.

**15**

Using a scalpel, make 2 cuts in the paw. Repeat steps 14–15 to make the other arm.

**16**

Glue the arms in position at the shoulders.

**17**

Remove the head from the body and use a pin tool to make 2 indents for the ears.

**18**

Using a cocktail stick, mark the outline for the top of the mouth as shown.

**19**

Use a scalpel to cut out the mouth and remove the fondant from inside the mouth.

**20**

Using a pointed colour shaper and the back of your thumb, soften and smooth out the lips and inside the mouth.

**21**

Roll 2 balls of beige fondant for the ears and make an indent in each one with a small ball tool.

**22**

Roll 2 small balls of pink fondant. Put some glue inside the indents you made in step 21 and attach the pink balls.

**23**

Glue the ears into the indents you made in step 17.

**24**

Roll out some light beige fondant. Using a tear cutter, cut out 2 shapes and remove the tips – these will form the muzzle around the mouth.

25 If the pieces are too large, slice off some of the fondant with the cutter.

26 You should be left with 2 shapes which meet in the middle and mirror each other as shown.

27 Glue the shapes above the mouth, covering the top lip. Make holes with a pin tool to represent whiskers. (To make it easier to work on the face, sit the head back on the body.)

28 To make the nose, roll a ball of brown fondant and pinch it between your thumb and finger to make a soft-pointed triangle.

29 Glue the nose in position so the bottom point touches the top of the mouth.

30 Roll 2 equal-sized white balls to make the eyes. Glue them into position and press flat. For lions, oval eyes work better than round eyes.

31 Roll 2 eyebrow shapes and glue them to the tops of the eyes. Make an indent in each eye with a small ball tool, for the pupils.

32 Roll 2 tiny balls of black fondant for the pupils and glue in place. At this point, glue the head in position.

33 For the mane, cut 3 strips of brown fondant and glue in place as shown. (This method is much easier than trying to attach 1 long piece.)

34 Using a sharp pair of scissors, cut around the mane, thus disguising the lines from the individual pieces of fondant.

35 If you want your lion to have a thicker mane, add a second layer of hair behind the first in the same way.

36

37

38

For the tail, roll a ball of beige fondant into a sausage shape and slice off one end to create a flat edge.

Shape a ball of brown fondant into a cone and attach it to one end of the tail. Use a wheel tool to give the tail tip the texture of hair.

Glue the tail to the base of the lion so that he sits on it.

39

Brush some soft pink edible tint onto the lion's cheeks. Use light brown tint to shade under the arms and the darker creases in his body.

1    Leaves

Roll out some green florist paste on a non-stick board. Using a scalpel, cut out a freehand leaf shape.

2

Emboss the leaf in a leaf or orchid veiner, then twist. Leave to dry for at least 2 hours and ideally 24 hours. Repeat using other shades of green. Scatter around the lion.

Grass

1

In a tray, mix various shades of green paste food colouring with a little water until you have water-colour consistency. Paint onto dry fondant (*see Top Tip, right*).

TOP TIP
To paint onto fondant icing, mix paste food colouring with water and use as you would watercolours. Avoid the use of shortening when rolling out your fondant as this will prevent the paint from adhering to the icing.

# Fairy Friends

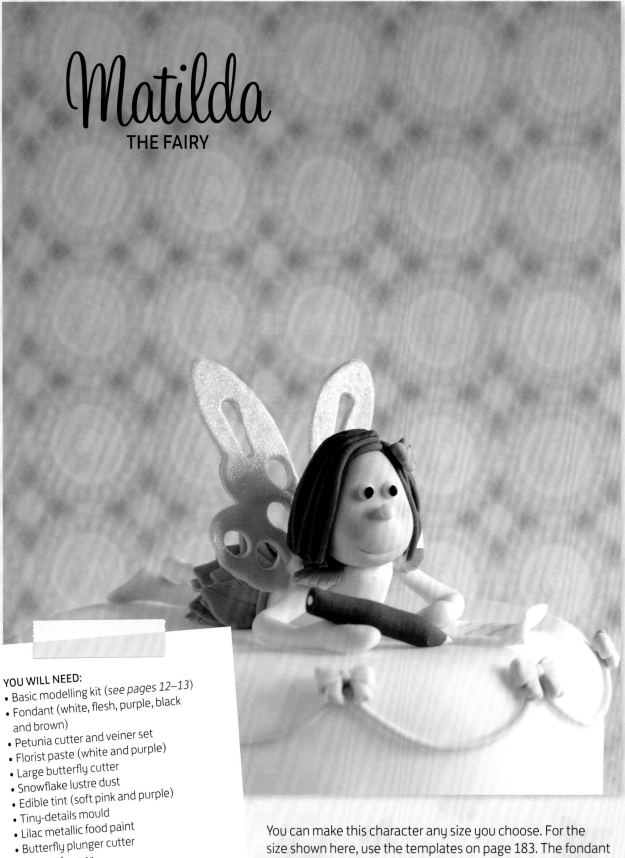

# Matilda
## THE FAIRY

**YOU WILL NEED:**
- Basic modelling kit (*see pages 12–13*)
- Fondant (white, flesh, purple, black and brown)
- Petunia cutter and veiner set
- Florist paste (white and purple)
- Large butterfly cutter
- Snowflake lustre dust
- Edible tint (soft pink and purple)
- Tiny-details mould
- Lilac metallic food paint
- Butterfly plunger cutter
- Sheet of paper
- Royal icing
- Endless garret frill cutter

You can make this character any size you choose. For the size shown here, use the templates on page 183. The fondant colours for Matilda are white, flesh, purple, black and brown. For the accessories you will need brown fondant and white and purple florist paste.

1

Roll a ball of white fondant for the body.

2

Shape the ball into a cone about 4 cm in length. Lay it on its side.

3

Turn up the narrower end of the cone slightly.

4

Push a length of spaghetti into the turned-up end of the fondant, leaving a short piece showing.

5

For the legs, roll 2 balls of flesh-coloured fondant. Shape each one into a long cone.

TOP TIP
When making a fairy, keep the underlying body and head quite small, as the clothing and hair will dramatically increase the overall size.

6

Take 1 leg and bend the bulbous end into a foot shape, creating a flat heel and pulling the toe area forward.

7

Turn the leg over and pinch the heel to make it narrower than the front of the foot.

8

Repeat steps 6–7 to make the other foot. Lay both legs with the feet facing downwards and pull the toes back a little.

9

Cross the legs and check that you have the toes pointing the right way.

10

Attach the legs to the back of the body using edible glue.

11

For the dress, roll out some purple fondant and cut out some flower shapes using a petunia cutter.

Fairy Friends 53

**12**

Line a petunia veiner with white vegetable fat to stop the fondant from sticking to it.

**13**

Place a petunia shape in the veiner and press.

**14**

Open the veiner and remove the flower using a soft brush.

**15**

Cut off all the petals, then remove all the pointed ends from the middle area.

**16**

Glue the petals around the body, overlapping them a little.

**17**

Add more petals, working up the body, until you reach the waist. Cover the final row with a thin length of fondant.

TOP TIP
When making fairies, you will often find that you need props to help their arms and legs stay in place. In the case of Matilda, her arms are not actually supporting her body – the body holds itself up. Take care to ensure that small limbs do not carry too much weight.

**18**

From the side, your fairy should look like this.

**19**

For the arms, roll 2 balls of flesh-coloured fondant and shape into cones. Flatten the bulbous ends.

**20**

Taking 1 arm, cut out a triangle from the flattened area to make a thumb. Smooth out the cut edges.

**21**

Put a small ball tool between the fingers and thumb, to make space to fit a pencil. Make 2 more petunia petals for the sleeves.

**22**

There is no need to make a thumb for the second hand. Glue the arms in place and cover the joins with the petal sleeves as shown.

**23**

Roll a sausage of white fondant and glue it along the fairy's back as shown.

**24**

Roll out some white florist paste and cut out a butterfly shape.

**25**

Cut off the wings, then remove the top and bottom sections as shown.

**26**

Cut out holes of different shapes and sizes, using a selection of nozzle tips.

**27**

Dust the wings with snowflake lustre dust.

**28**

Push the wings into the strip of white fondant. You shouldn't need glue, but, if you wish, you can add a little to each wing before attaching.

**29**

At this stage, your fairy should look like this.

**TOP TIP**
Never glue a fairy's head in position until the very end, as you will keep having to remove it in order to add clothing.

**30**

To make the head, roll a ball of flesh-coloured fondant. Mould into an egg shape.

**31**

To make the bridge of the nose, gently press with your right thumb to create an indent between 10 o'clock and 4 o'clock.

**32**

With your left thumb, make an indent between 2 o'clock and 8 o'clock as shown.

**33**

Roll a small ball of flesh-coloured fondant and glue it to the peak that you've created, to make the nose.

**34**

Use a pin tool to make 2 holes for the eyes.

**35**

Place the head on the fairy. With the wide end of a size 2 nozzle, make a smile, ensuring that it's not too low (hence, you add the head first).

**36**

Remove the head again, then attach 2 white fondant balls to make the eyes. Press them flat as you glue them in place.

**37**

For the pupils, roll 2 tiny balls of black fondant and glue them onto the eyes. Alternatively, use black non-pareils.

**38**

Dust the cheeks with pink edible tint, using a small soft brush.

**39**

Glue the head in place and add glue to the scalp.

**40**

Put some brown fondant into a craft gun with a hair nozzle attached, then squeeze to produce brown hair.

**41**

Lay the craft gun flat on the work surface, then cut the hair away using scissors.

**TOP TIP**
When making hair using fondant and a craft gun, ensure that you arrange the hair in its final position before it dries. Once the thin strands of fondant dry, they will become very fragile and will snap if moved.

**42**

Glue some hair over one side of the head.

**43**

Glue hair onto the other side.

**44**

Cut the hair to your desired length.

45

With purple florist paste or fondant, make a tiny bow using a bow mould.

46

Bend the mould back to release the bow.

47

Glue the bow to the hair as shown.

**Pencil and paper**

1

To make a pencil, roll a sausage of brown fondant and cut to the required length.

2

Cut 1 end into a point. Keep the cut fairly rough, so that it looks handmade.

3

Paint the tip of the pencil with lilac metallic food paint.

4

Put a dot of paint at the other end of the pencil, for the base of the pencil lead. Put the pencil in the fairy's hand.

TOP TIP
To make the fairies look petite, it is a good idea to use oversized accessories. Giant pencils, cotton reels and books all work well.

5

Cut out a rectangle of white florist paste. Ruffle the edges and paint wavy lines using lilac metallic food paint.

### Butterflies

**1**

Roll out some purple florist paste and cut out some butterfly shapes using a plunger cutter.

**2**

Bend the butterflies in the middle and place them in folded paper. Leave to dry for at least 2 hours and ideally overnight.

**3**

When the butterflies are dry, dust with purple edible tint.

**4**

Use royal icing to attach the butterflies to the side of your cake, then pipe 3 little dots of royal icing along the middle of each one, to make the body.

### Swags and border

**1**

Pipe lines of florist paste around the cake using a size 1 piping nozzle or a craft gun. If using the latter, glue the paste at each drop. Make some little bows, using a bow mould, to cover the joins.

**2**

For the border, roll out some purple fondant and, using an endless garrett cutter, cut out a wide frill long enough to go all the way around the cake.

**3**

Glue the frill around the base of the cake as shown.

### CAKE DESIGN

Here, I placed Matilda on a cake measuring about 12 cm in diameter and 15 cm in depth. This gave enough space for some decoration on the sides of the cake. With fairies, I try to match the flavour of the cake to the colour of the fairy. In this case, I added a subtle lavender flavouring to the buttercream.

# Eden
## THE FAIRY

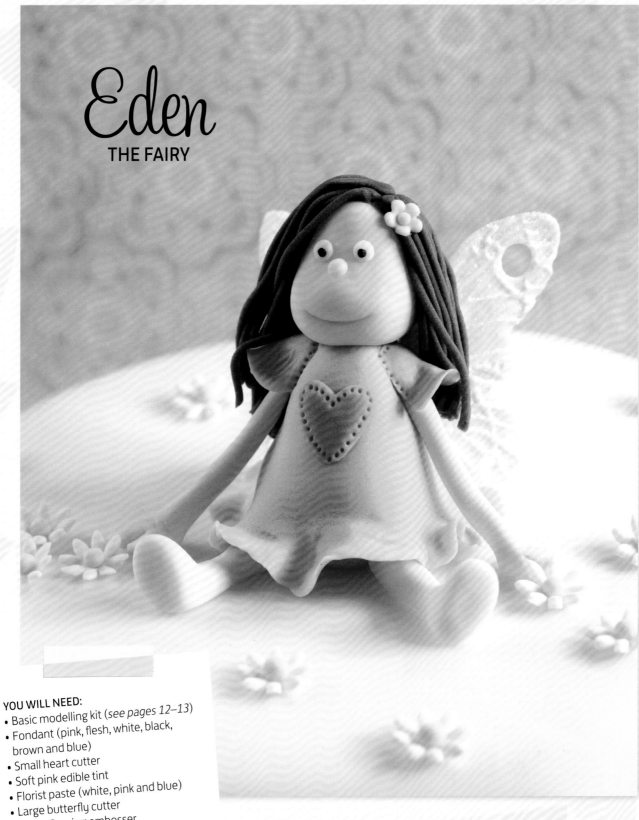

**YOU WILL NEED:**
- Basic modelling kit (*see pages 12–13*)
- Fondant (pink, flesh, white, black, brown and blue)
- Small heart cutter
- Soft pink edible tint
- Florist paste (white, pink and blue)
- Large butterfly cutter
- Butterfly wing embosser
- Snowflake lustre dust
- Small blossom cutter

You can make this character any size you choose. For the size shown here, use the templates on page 182. The fondant colours for Eden are pink, flesh, white, black and brown. For the accessories you will need white and blue fondant, and white, pink and blue florist paste.

1

Roll a ball of pink fondant for the body and a flesh-coloured ball for the head.

2

Roll the pink ball into a cone and insert a length of spaghetti as shown.

3

Roll the flesh-coloured fondant into an egg shape. Uniquely, a fairy's mouth is at the larger end.

**TOP TIP**
When working with 3-dimensional figures, resist the urge to draw on features, as these will be 2-dimensional and won't look as good as if they're moulded.

4

Press with your right thumb to create an indent between 10 o'clock and 4 o'clock.

5

With your left thumb, make an indent between 2 o'clock and 8 o'clock as shown.

6

You're aiming for the shape on the left. Try not to get the angle wrong or press too hard.

7

Roll a small ball of flesh-coloured fondant and glue it to the peak that you've created, to make the nose.

8

Using the wide end of a size 2 nozzle, make

9

Use a pin tool to make 2 holes for the eyes. Make sure everything is in the correct place and in proportion before you proceed.

10

Position the head on the spaghetti (don't glue it) and glue on 2 white balls for the eyes. Press them flat.

11

Glue 2 black fondant balls onto the eyes, for the pupils, or use black non-pareils.

12

For the legs, roll 2 flesh-coloured balls into sausages, keeping a ball at 1 end.

13

Take 1 leg and pinch up the bulbous end to make a foot shape. Don't make it too flat.

14

Pinch the base of the foot so that the ankle end is thinner than the toe end.

15. Repeat steps 13–14 to make the other leg, then glue both legs to the body.

16. To make the dress, roll out some pink fondant (or florist paste, if you find this easier to work with) and cut out a piece with a wavy line along the base.

17. Pinch the edge of the fondant or paste to give it a frilled effect.

18. Glue the dress around the body, with the join at the back. Roughly smooth out the seam with your finger (this will be covered).

**TOP TIP**
Where possible, try to make your fairy clothes from fondant, as it will be nice to eat. If the dress is very fiddly, you can use florist paste, or half fondant and half florist paste. This will make the paste firmer and therefore easier to work with.

19. When the dress is in place, gently shape the skirt using a soft brush.

20. Cut out a heart from a darker pink fondant and glue this to the front of the dress.

21. Using a pin tool, mark dots around the outside of the heart to resemble stitching.

22. For the arms, roll 2 balls of fondant, just as you did for the legs, but smaller.

23. Take 1 arm and pinch the bulbous end as shown, to make a hand.

24. Using a scalpel, cut a small triangular piece out of the hand to make a thumb.

25. Soften the edges of the thumb and the hand.

26. Repeat steps 23–5 to complete the other arm, then glue the arms in place.

27. To make the sleeves, cut out 2 pieces of fondant as shown.

**28**

Glue the sleeves to the tops of the arms (*see Top Tip, below right*).

**29**

Mark dots around the sleeves, using a pin tool.

**30**

At this stage, you can glue on the head.

**31**

Gently dust the cheeks with pink edible tint, using a size 1 or 2 brush.

**32**

Cover the head with edible glue, ready to attach the hair (starting at the back of the head).

**33**

Make hair using brown fondant and a craft gun with a hair nozzle. For details about using a craft gun, see page 56.

**TOP TIP**
If the sleeves are sitting too flat on the arms, place a small ball of fondant underneath each one before gluing them to the arms.

**34**

Glue the second bunch of hair on one side of the head.

**35**

Attach a third bunch of hair on the other side of the head.

**36**

Use scissors to cut the hair as you wish.

**37**

Using edible glue, attach a small flower to the hair.

**38**

To make the wings, roll out some white florist paste and cut out a butterfly shape.

**39**

Cut off the wings, then remove the bottom tips.

**40**

Emboss the wings by pressing them in a butterfly wing embosser.

**41** Cut out holes of different sizes, using a selection of nozzle tips.

**42** Dust the wings with snowflake lustre dust.

**43** Glue the wings in place in between the central strands of hair. If the wings need extra support, glue a ball of fondant to the fairy's back, then glue the wings to that.

**44** Your finished fairy should look like this.

**Bunting**

**1** You'll need a craft gun and a nozzle with a single hole in it. Fill the gun with pink florist paste.

**2** Pipe long lines of paste and glue them to the side of the cake at the beginning and end of each length.

**3** Cut a series of triangles from florist paste.

**4** Glue the triangles along the base of the lengths of paste.

**5** Use small flowers to cover the joins between the lengths of paste.

**CAKE DESIGN**
For the picture opposite, I made a cake of approximately 18 cm in diameter and 10 cm in depth. This allows enough room to decorate the sides with bunting. You could add more small daisy flowers to the cake board if you wish.

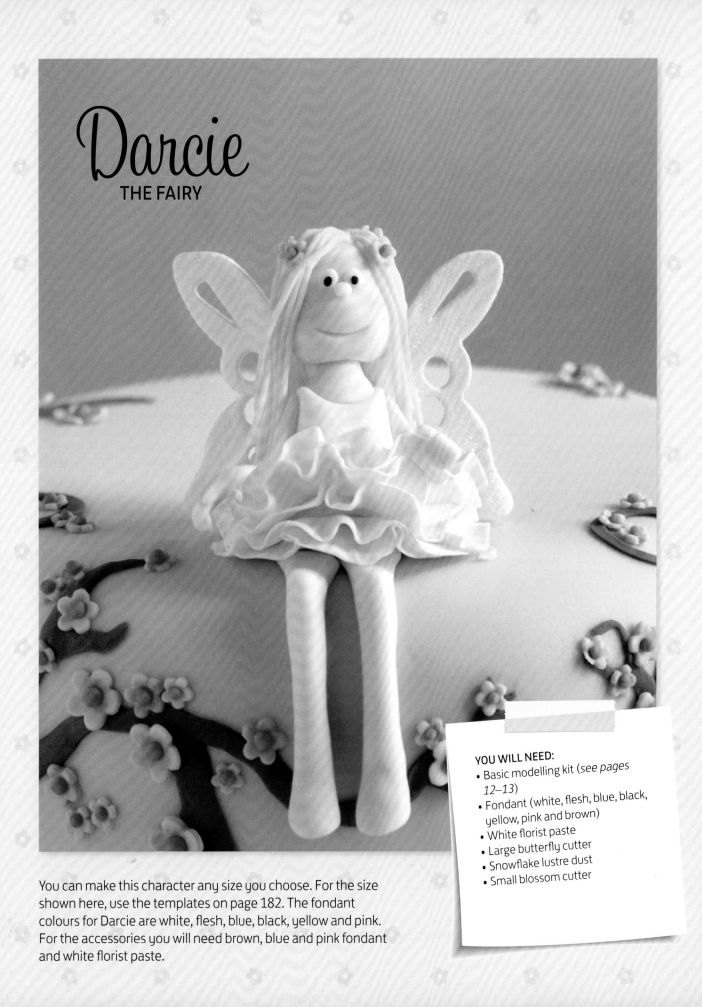

# Darcie
## THE FAIRY

You can make this character any size you choose. For the size shown here, use the templates on page 182. The fondant colours for Darcie are white, flesh, blue, black, yellow and pink. For the accessories you will need brown, blue and pink fondant and white florist paste.

**YOU WILL NEED:**
- Basic modelling kit (*see pages 12–13*)
- Fondant (white, flesh, blue, black, yellow, pink and brown)
- White florist paste
- Large butterfly cutter
- Snowflake lustre dust
- Small blossom cutter

1

Roll a ball of white fondant into a cone shape.

2

Lay the cone on its side and, using an oval cutter that's narrower than the top of your cone, cut out a third of an oval shape.

3

Using your finger and thumb, smooth out the cut area to ensure there are no jagged edges.

4

To create a neck, roll a flesh-coloured ball of fondant and shape it into a cone.

5

Flatten the cone a little, so it's about 5 mm thick.

**TOP TIP**
It's a good idea to make the fairy's body the same colour as the clothing (rather than flesh colour), as, typically, the body doubles up as the dress.

6

Cut off and discard the narrow end, then glue the neck into the curve made in step 2.

7

Push a length of spaghetti through the body, down to the base of the fondant.

8

To make the legs, roll 2 balls of flesh-coloured fondant into long cones as shown.

9

Take 1 leg and pinch up the bulbous end to create a foot.

10

Bend the leg about halfway along, to create a knee. Repeat steps 9 and 10 to make the other leg.

11

Position the legs on the edge of your cake. You may need to remove some fondant from the tops of the legs.

12

Once you're happy with the positioning, gently lift each leg to glue it in place on the cake.

**13**

Position the body behind the legs and glue in place.

**14**

Cut a circle of white florist paste (about 5 cm in diameter). It should be big enough to make a skirt, but not so big that it covers the knees.

**15**

Use a petal veiner to ruffle the edges of the paste.

TOP TIP
It's easiest to make very frilly dresses using florist paste, or half florist paste and half fondant.

**16**

Once your paste circle is fully ruffled, cut out a circle from the centre. This should be about the same diamater as the body.

**17**

Slide this layer of the skirt down the body until it sits on the legs. Apply a line of glue above this layer.

**18**

Repeat steps 14–17 to make 4 more layers (or more if you wish), to build up a tutu.

**19**

Your fairy should now look like this.

**20**

For the arms, roll 2 balls of flesh-coloured fondant and shape into cones.

**21**

Take 1 hand, flatten the palm slightly and cut out a piece to make a thumb.

**22**

Soften the edges of the thumb and the hand.

**23**

Bend the arm, then tuck the fingers in, as though they're gripping. Repeat steps 21–3 for the other arm, making it more relaxed.

**24**

Glue on the arms at the shoulders – the left hand should be gripping the dress. If the neck seems too long, trim it with a scalpel.

**25**

Cut a butterfly shape from white florist paste.

**26**

Cut off the wings, then remove the top sections as shown.

**27**

Make different-shaped holes in the wings, using nozzle tips or cutters. Dust with snowflake lustre dust.

**28**

Glue the wings onto the body (*see Top Tip, right*).

**TOP TIP**
If the wings need more support, roll a ball of fondant and glue this to the back using royal icing. Then use more royal icing to attach the wings to the fondant (it will be covered by hair).

**29**

To make the head, roll a flesh-coloured ball of fondant into an egg shape.

**30**

Press with your right thumb to make an indent between 10 o'clock and 4 o'clock.

**31**

With your left thumb, make an indent between 2 o'clock and 8 o'clock, to form a peak.

**32**

Roll a small ball and glue it to the peak, to make the nose. Mark 2 eyes with a pin tool.

**33**

Make the mouth with the wider end of a piping nozzle.

**34**

Roll 2 white fondant balls for the eyes and glue in place. Add 2 black fondant balls for pupils.

**35**

Glue the head in place.

**36**

Apply glue to the top of the head.

**37**

Make the hair using yellow fondant and a craft gun with a hair nozzle attached.

Cover the head with yellow hair.

Cut the hair to the desired length, using a small pair of scissors.

Roll out some pale pink fondant and cut out 6 or 7 small blossoms. Glue little dark pink balls into the centres.

Glue the flowers around the head.

Using a size 1 or 2 brush, dust the cheeks with soft pink edible tint.

Your finished fairy should look like this.

**Blossom tree**

Cut some strips of brown fondant into various curved and staight shapes, to make the branches.

Glue the branches around the sides of your cake.

Decorate with blossom flowers to match the fairy's hair. You can fix these in place using edible glue or royal icing.

CAKE DESIGN
The cake shown here measures about 20 cm in diameter by 12 cm in depth. You can make the blossom as elaborate or as simple as you wish, covering the entire cake and board if you wish, or just the top of the cake. This fairy would also work well sitting on a fondant-topped cupcake with a similar design to that shown here.

# Bramble & Ben

## THE FAIRIES

You can make these characters any size you choose. For the sizes shown here, use the templates on page 183. The fondant colours for these fairies are pink, blue, flesh, white, black, yellow and orange. For the accessories you will need brown, red, white and green fondant.

**YOU WILL NEED:**

- Basic modelling kit (*see pages 12–13*)
- Fondant (pink, blue, brown, flesh, white, black, yellow, orange, red and green)
- Carnation cutter set
- Butterfly cutter
- Leaf veiner
- Sheet of paper
- Snowflake or pink lustre dust
- Soft pink edible tint
- Small blossom cutter
- Calyx cutter set
- Orange or pink edible ink pen
- Green royal icing

Roll 2 large balls – 1 in pink fondant and 1 in blue – for the bodies.

Roll the balls into cones, about 4 cm in height.

To make the log seat, roll a sausage of brown fondant, about 3 cm in diameter and 15 cm in length.

Pinch the paste at each end of the log, to make a rim.

Roll a wheel tool along the log to create a bark effect. The lines shouldn't be straight.

**TOP TIP**
When making a number of fairies, it's a good idea to roll all the bodies at the same time, then all the heads, and so on. This will help you to remember the sizes and therefore work quicker.

To make the legs, roll 4 balls of flesh-coloured fondant into cones as shown.

Take 1 leg and pinch up the bulbous end to create a foot shape.

Pinch the back of the foot, so the ankle is narrower than the toe end.

Bend the leg to make a knee.

Before you position the first leg, push 2 lengths of spaghetti into the log where the fairies will sit.

Glue the leg of Ben the boy onto the log, shortening it if necessary.

Repeat steps 7–11 to make Ben's other leg. Make Bramble's legs in the same way but slightly longer. Glue her first leg at an angle.

Position her second leg crossing over the first leg as shown, then glue in place.

Once you're happy with the legs, slide the bodies onto the spaghetti and glue in place on the log.

To make Ben's outfit, roll out a long strip of blue fondant and cut out a row of triangles to make a zig zag.

Paint a line of glue around the base of his body and glue on the outfit as shown.

Using a pin tool, make dots along the edges of the zig zag to resemble stitching.

TOP TIP
When making fairy wings, experiment with different butterfly cutters and veiners. You can also use leaf cutters to create long, spiral or pointed wings.

To make Bramble's dress, roll out some pink fondant and cut out a carnation shape using a cutter.

Ruffle the edges of the carnation with a cocktail stick.

Cut out the centre using a number 2 nozzle.

Slide the carnation frill over the girl's body, then apply a line of glue on the top.

Repeat steps 18–21 to make 3 or 4 more layers. Stick each one to the glue underneath. Adjust the ruffles with a cocktail stick or soft brush.

**23**

For the outside arms, roll 2 flesh-coloured cones and flatten the bulbous ends.

**24**

Take each arm and bend to make an elbow. Press the palm a little.

**25**

Attach the arms as shown, using edible glue. Add a small ball of fondant at the top of Bramble's arm.

**26**

Make another carnation shape, as in steps 18–20, then cut out 2 small sections.

**27**

Glue 1 piece over the ball of fondant at the top of the arm, to make a sleeve. Put the other piece to one side.

**28**

For the inside arms, roll 2 cones and flatten the wider ends. Take 1 arm, cut out a piece to make a thumb and smooth out the edges.

**TOP TIP**
For very small fairies, don't try to cut individual fingers. It will look neater if you just indicate fingers and a thumb.

**29**

Take the other arm, for Bramble, and cut a thumb on the other side of the hand. Attach the sleeve.

**30**

Glue the arms in position, bending them so the hands touch. Glue the hands together.

**31**

Roll out some pink fondant and cut out a butterfly shape for Bramble's wings.

**32**

Emboss the butterfly in a leaf veiner.

**33**

Fold a sheet of paper into a concertina and place the butterfly on the paper as shown. Leave to dry for at least 2 hours and ideally overnight.

**34**

Dust the butterfly with snowflake or pink lustre dust.

**35** Glue the wings in place on Bramble's back, using edible glue or royal icing.

**36** Your fairies should now look like this.

**37** For the heads, roll 2 balls of flesh-coloured fondant and mould into egg shapes.

**38** Take 1 head and press with your right thumb to make an indent between 10 o'clock and 4 o'clock.

**39** With your left thumb, make an indent between 2 o'clock and 8 o'clock, to form a peak.

**40** Roll a small ball of fondant and glue it to the peak, to make the nose. Mark 2 eyes with a pin tool.

**41** Use the wider end of a nozzle to make a smile.

**42** For eyes, glue on 2 white balls and flatten. Glue the head onto the girl's body, then add pupils.

**43** Put yellow fondant in a craft gun with a hair nozzle. Make long strips, gluing in place.

**44** Cut the hair with a small pair of scissors.

**45** Using a small brush, dust her cheeks with soft pink edible tint.

**46** Use a cutter to cut out a tiny blossom flower and glue it to Bramble's hair.

**47** To complete the boy, roll out some blue fondant and cut out a blue calyx shape, using a calyx cutter.

**48** Glue this onto the neck, pushing it down over the spaghetti, to cover the join between the arms and the body.

**49**

Gently press down the calyx ends, and twist it a little if it isn't fully covering the arms.

**50**

Make another head, following steps 38–42, then glue it to the boy's body.

**51**

Make ears by rolling 2 tiny balls and indenting the centres with a small ball tool.

**52**

Glue the ears in place on the sides of Ben's head.

**53**

Your fairies should now look like this.

**54**

Put bright orange fondant into a craft gun with a hair nozzle, and put a little glue onto the head. Pipe some hair onto the glue.

**55**

Let the hair fall so that it's messy, then cut it very short. Add freckles, using an orange or pink edible ink pen.

**56**

Your finished fairies should look like this. Leave them to dry for at least 24 hours, then move them to your cake, keeping them in position on the log.

### Spike the Hedgehog

To make a hedgehog, roll a ball of brown fondant into a cone and rest it on the work surface to make a flat base.

Make tiny cuts in the fondant, starting a little way along the cone and working up the body.

Add tiny eyes (using the same techniques as for the fairies) and a little ball of red fondant for a nose.

### Grass

For the grass, cut out pointed strips of fondant in different shades of green, and glue them around the sides of the cake.

Pipe green royal icing around the base to cover the edge of the cake.

**TOP TIP**
Cover any messy joins with piping or ribbon. Here, I have used a grass nozzle to cover the join between the cake and the drum. If you damage the cake or make a mistake, use a carefully positioned flower or animal to cover the error.

### Toadstools

Roll a ball of red fondant into a cone.

Cut off the rounded end. The pointed end will make the top of the toadstool.

For the stalk, roll a sausage of white fondant and cut off both ends.

Glue the white stalk to the base of the red cone and cover in white fondant spots, pressing them flat. Repeat to make more toadstools.

**CAKE DESIGN**
For the picture opposite, I made a round cake of about 20 cm in diameter and 10 cm in depth. The fairies are sitting in an enchanted forest, so you could use a larger cake to allow for other animals, including hedgehogs, rabbits and even elves. You could also decorate the cake board with smaller animals such as ladybirds and butterflies. I like to use little toadstools, flowers and hedgehogs as filler elements on cupcakes.

# Monsters and Aliens

# BLinky
## THE ALIEN

You can make this character any size you choose. For the size shown here, use the templates on page 184. The fondant colours for Blinky are purple, white, yellow, red, black and pink. You will need the same colours for the accessories.

YOU WILL NEED:
- Basic modelling kit (see pages 12–13)
- Fondant (purple, white, yellow, red, black and pink)
- Purple edible tint
- Snowflake lustre dust
- Kitchen paper

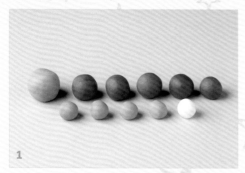

1

Roll 5 equal-sized balls of dark purple fondant, 1 larger ball and 4 smaller balls of light purple and 1 small white ball.

2

Roll each dark purple ball to make a sausage 5 mm in diameter and the lengths shown on the template. Wrap the other balls in a plastic bag.

3

Curve the largest sausage and glue the ends together. Use the pointed colour shaper to soften the join.

4

Repeat step 3 for the other sausages. The loops will get progressively smaller. Glue them one on top of the other.

5

Roll the larger light purple ball into an egg shape, to make the head. Glue into the hole at the top of the body.

6

Using a size 2 nozzle, make a groove in the correct position for a smiling mouth.

7

Push a large ball tool into the head, to make an eye shape. Press the index finger of your free hand against the fondant on top of the ball tool to make a lip over the eye socket.

8

Using a cocktail stick, make an open mouth ready for the tongue to sit in.

Take the small ball of white fondant and cut in half with a scalpel.

10

Shape 1 of the halves so it is smooth and round and push it into the eye socket, gluing in place.

11

Cut out small circles of yellow and red fondant and roll a small ball of black fondant. These must be small enough to fit on the white eye.

12

Glue on the yellow fondant circle, then the red, and push down with the flat-ended colour shaper so they're flush with the white fondant.

**13** Glue on the black ball and push down with the flat-ended colour shaper.

**14** Add a tiny ball of white fondant to the eye.

**15** Take 2 of the small light purple balls and press down with the side of your thumb to create a flat half.

**16** Apply glue to the flat half of each piece and slot underneath the body.

**17** Make 3 holes in each foot using the pointed colour shaper.

**18** Use a cocktail stick to make a slot in each side of the upper body, ready for the arms.

**19** Take the remaining 2 light purple balls and roll them into long cone shapes.

**20** Cut a small thumb slit in each cone.

**21** Take 1 cone and, using your fingertip, smooth out the thumb and fingers to look like a mitten.

**22** Bend the arm to make an elbow and curve the hand around so the fingers tuck into the palm.

**23** Wrap the thumb over the top of the fingers.

**24** Repeat steps 21–3 to make the other arm, then secure both arms in the slots created in step 18 and glue in place.

**25** Cut 2 small strips of red fondant, then wrap them around the tops of the arms to cover any messy joins.

**26** Using a cocktail stick, make a row of tiny holes along each red strip to resemble armour.

**27**

Using red fondant, roll 3 tiny cone shapes. They should be very thin and pointy.

**28**

Glue the cones to the top of the head. Once fixed in place, bend the ends with your fingertips to make them curl.

**31**

Brush dark purple edible tint into all the holes in the toes and around the rings of the body.

**29**

Cut out a teardrop shape of light pink fondant and slice off the point. Make a groove with the back of a scalpel.

**30**

Put some glue into the hole you made for the mouth in step 8 and push in the tongue.

## Doogi

**1**

Roll a purple ball, about 2 cm in diameter, and shape into a cone. Cut in half, from the top to the centre, as shown.

**2**

Round off the edges of the cut with your fingers and insert a length of spaghetti in each side.

**3**

Roll 2 balls of purple fondant and push them onto the protruding pieces of spaghetti, gluing in place. Make an indent in each ball with a large ball tool.

**4**

Create texture all over the body by gently making marks using an angle chisel colour shaper.

**5**

For legs and arms, make 4 long cones and flatten the wide ends. Bend as shown and glue in place.

**6**

Make 2 eyes following steps 9–14 for Blinky, then you have a little matching friend.

## Slugger

**1**

Slugger is made using the principles you applied to Blinky. Roll 9 purple fondant balls decreasing in size.

**2**

Glue the balls together, then add a tenth ball to make a head/eye, with 3 small balls on top. Indent the balls with a ball tool as shown.

**3**

Make 1 eye following steps 9–14 for Blinky, then add 2 legs (*see Doogi, step 5*). Make 4 tiny red cones and glue into the indents.

Rocky

**1**

Using purple fondant, roll an oval shape and cut it through the middle from the top to halfway down.

**2**

Pinch the fondant between your finger and a large ball tool to create 2 eye sockets.

**3**

For the legs, roll 4 balls of purple fondant into long sausages.

**4**

Take 1 leg and bend as shown. Pinch at both ends. The larger end is the foot.

**5**

Repeat step 4 to create 4 legs, then make 2 holes in the front of each foot with a pin tool.

**6**

Glue the legs in place as shown.

**7**

Create eyes following steps 9–14 for Blinky, then roll tiny cones of red fondant to make little spikes. Glue them in place as shown.

Satin white planet

**1**

On your board or cake, add lumps of fondant to create little mountain bumps.

**2**

Cover the board or cake with white fondant.

**3**

Mix snowflake lustre dust with dipping solution (*see page 9*) and paint onto the fondant.

**4**

To create texture, press a crumpled sheet of kitchen paper all over the fondant.

CAKE DESIGN
Blinky and his friends can be used to decorate any cake, cake board, cake tiers or individual cupcakes. The latter works very well as each cupcake is related but slightly different. You can create a satin white planet effect on a large cake, mini cake or cupcake surface.

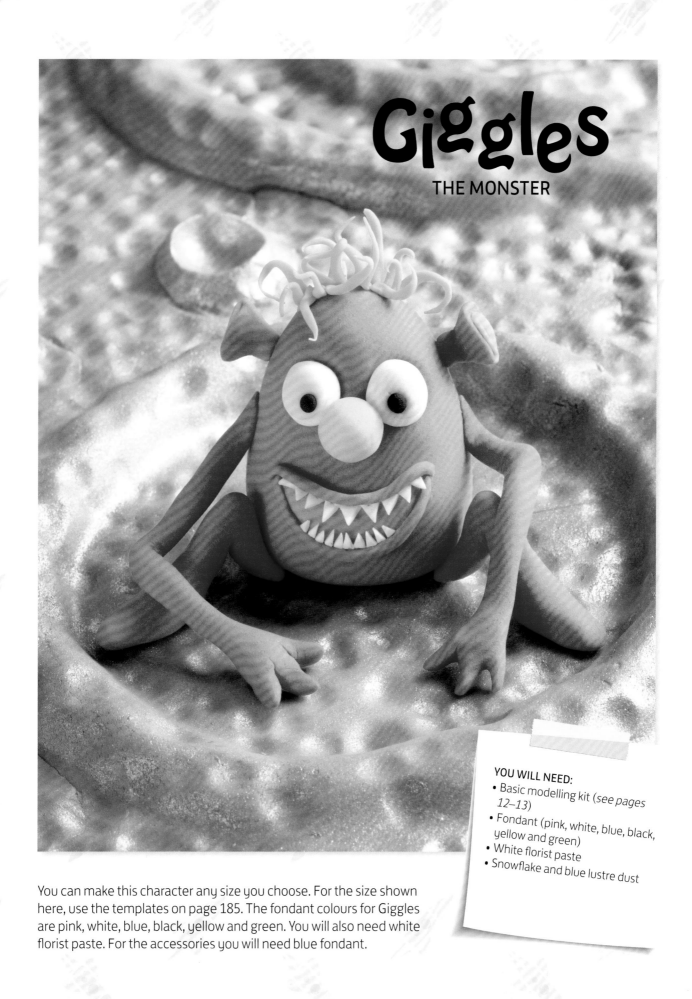

# Giggles

## THE MONSTER

**YOU WILL NEED:**
- Basic modelling kit (*see pages 12–13*)
- Fondant (pink, white, blue, black, yellow and green)
- White florist paste
- Snowflake and blue lustre dust

You can make this character any size you choose. For the size shown here, use the templates on page 185. The fondant colours for Giggles are pink, white, blue, black, yellow and green. You will also need white florist paste. For the accessories you will need blue fondant.

To make the body, roll a large ball of pink fondant.

Roll the ball into an egg shape.

Using a tear cutter about 3 cm in length, cut out a lighter pink fondant shape.

Cut off the pointed end of the tear shape.

Using the round end of the cutter, cut a crescent from the flat side to make a smiling mouth.

Glue the mouth to the body.

Using more lighter pink fondant, roll 2 long thin sausages. Glue one around the bottom of the mouth, and the other around the top.

Trim off the ends with a scalpel.

Make indents for the eyes and nose using a ball tool.

TOP TIP
By having one feature that stands out more than any other, you will find it easier to create a personality for your character. Choose what attribute is the most representative and make that the main focus.

For the eyes, roll 2 white balls and press flat. Roll 2 smaller pale blue balls, flatten and glue to the whites, then add 2 tiny black balls for the pupils.

Glue the eyes into the indents created in step 9.

Using yellow fondant, roll a large ball for the nose and glue in position.

For the teeth, roll out some white florist paste until very thin, then cut out some tiny triangles.

Glue the teeth inside the mouth along the top and bottom lips.

For the hair, roll about 8 thin pointy lengths of green fondant.

Glue the hair onto the top of the head.

Your monster should look like this.

To make the ears, roll 2 balls of pink fondant and form into cone shapes.

Take 1 cone and push a large ball tool into the wider end to make an indent.

Roll a small circle of lighter pink fondant and press it into the indent.

Cut off the point of the cone. Repeat steps 19–21 to make the second ear.

Push a short length of spaghetti into each side of the head to support the ears.

Put some edible glue onto the base of each ear, then push the ears onto the spaghetti supports, making sure they stick to the sides of the head.

For the legs, roll 2 balls of pink fondant and shape into sausages, leaving a bulbous section at one end about 1 cm long.

Take 1 leg and bend it to create a knee as shown.

Repeat step 25 to make the other leg, then glue both legs underneath the body so your monster is sitting on the legs.

To make the arms, roll 2 balls of pink fondant and shape into sausages with a ball at 1 end.

Take 1 arm and, using a scalpel, cut out 2 small triangles to create 3 fingers as shown.

Bend the arm to create an elbow, then smooth out the edges of the fingers between your thumb and finger.

Repeat steps 28–9 to make the second arm, then glue both arms in place, below the ears but higher than the mouth.

Your finished monster should look like this.

**Diplet**

Make a pink droplet shape and add a face as you did for Giggles (*see steps 3–14*). Make 2 small droplets for the feet and 2 flattened balls for the arms.

Attach a green fondant curl to either side to make the hair.

**Peewee and Zilla**

To make Peewee and Zilla, or other characters, combine any of the techniques used to make Giggles, and adapt them for each new monster.

**Landscape**

Roll sausages of fondant and place them on a cake board or cake surface to make craters.

Cover the surface with blue fondant and make a bumpy texture using a small ball tool. To make a small crater, attach a blue ball to the surface and push down inside using a large ball tool, pressing the fondant against your finger to create a thin lip.

Mix snowflake and blue lustre dust with a few drops of dipping solution (*see page 9*) and paint over the surface.

To create the water, use piping gel mixed with a few drops of blue paste food colouring.

**CAKE DESIGN**
Putting a monster or alien on a cake is a great opportunity to experiment with texture. Here, I have created a texture for the surface of a swamp or planet. This can be made on a cake, or on a board with the cake itself as the planet. If you intend to create bumps on the surface of the cake, ensure your fondant is quite thick and chill the cake before working so it doesn't change shape when you apply pressure to the surface.

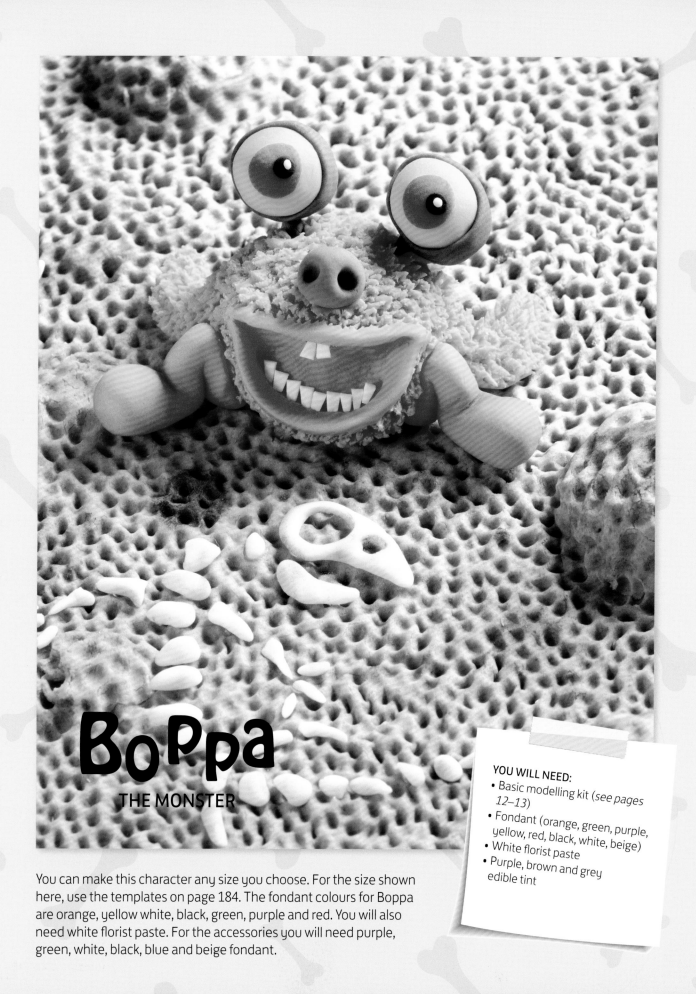

# BoPPa

## THE MONSTER

You can make this character any size you choose. For the size shown here, use the templates on page 184. The fondant colours for Boppa are orange, yellow white, black, green, purple and red. You will also need white florist paste. For the accessories you will need purple, green, white, black, blue and beige fondant.

**YOU WILL NEED:**
- Basic modelling kit (*see pages 12–13*)
- Fondant (orange, green, purple, yellow, red, black, white, beige)
- White florist paste
- Purple, brown and grey edible tint

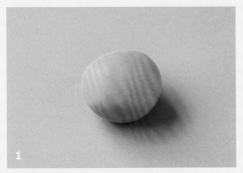

1

Roll a large ball of orange fondant for the body.

2

Using a scalpel, cut out a semi-circle to create a mouth.

3

Cut away the inside of the mouth.

4

Using your finger and thumb, pinch around the edge of the semi-circle to create the lips.

5

Use a flat-ended colour shaper to smooth down any rough areas and gently press around the inside edge of the mouth.

6

To make the arms, roll 2 orange balls and flatten into crescent shapes. They should bend in the middle to resemble paddles or flippers.

7

Attach the arms to the body using edible glue.

8

Using the tip of a pair of scissors, cut tiny snips into the body and the arms to create a furry texture.

9

Thinly roll out a piece of florist paste, then cut out small triangles with one end cut off to make teeth.

10

Glue the teeth inside the mouth, about 2 mm in.

11

Roll a ball of green fondant for the nose, and make 2 indents with a small ball tool for the nostrils.

12

Dust inside the nostrils with purple edible tint.

**13**

Glue the nose in place above the mouth. Using a pin tool, make 2 holes for the eyes.

**14**

To make the legs, roll 2 balls of orange fondant into sausage shapes with a ball at 1 end.

**15**

Take 1 leg and bend it in the middle to create a knee.

**16**

The angle of the bend should be increased as shown, making a foot at the ball end and a length of fondant at the other end.

**17**

Repeat steps 15–16 to make the other leg, then cut off the leftover fondant as shown.

**18**

Glue both legs in place underneath the monster.

**TOP TIP**
When making monsters, try to work with complementary colours. These will naturally stand out and give your cake great impact.

**19**

For the eyes, roll 2 balls of purple fondant. Make a hollow in each ball using a ball tool, then push the edge of the fondant against your finger with the tool to create a lip.

**20**

Roll 2 balls of yellow fondant and cut off 1 third of each ball.

**21**

Glue the larger yellow pieces into the cavities made in the purple eye sockets.

**22**

Cut out 2 red circles, glue 2 black balls on top and add 2 tiny white balls. Glue onto the yellow eyes. Smooth the edges with a flat-ended colour shaper.

**23**

Wrap purple fondant around a piece of spaghetti as shown, then glue the tip into a purple eye socket. Repeat for the other eye.

Push the eyes into the holes made in step 13 (you may need to put a little glue into the holes).

TOP TIP
When working with fondant, keep your finger nails short. It is very easy to dent a finished character with a sharp or long nail. It is also much easier to model with shorter finger nails, as most modelling is performed using the tips of your fingers.

Your finished monster should look like this.

Landscape

Place some uneven lumps of fondant around your cake or board (glue in place using cooled boiled water). Brush your board with water.

Cover the cake or board with beige fondant about 5 mm thick.

Use the small end of a ball tool to create a rock texture all over the surface of the fondant.

Dust the textured surface with brown edible tint.

Bones

For the bones, use white fondant to make a selection of randomly shaped pieces, then dust with grey edible tint.

Arrange the bones on the cake or board to create a skeleton shape.

### Boggle the purple monster

**1** Roll a ball of purple fondant into a long pointed sausage, leaving a ball at 1 end.

**2** Make 3 indents for the eye sockets with a ball tool, and mark on the mouth using the tip of a scalpel or a size 2 nozzle.

**3** Add green patches to the monster and smooth down with a flat-ended colour shaper.

**4** To make the eyes, roll 3 white balls, glue on flat green circles, then top with tiny black balls. Make the teeth using florist paste.

**5** Glue the eyes and teeth in place using edible glue.

### Sludge the green monster

**1** Roll a ball of green fondant into a pointed cone shape.

**2** Make a spine by pinching the pointed end between your thumb and finger.

**3** Roll a green ball for the head and make 2 indents for the eyes. Roll 2 small white balls and add pupils. Roll a small green ball for the nose. Make a smile with a size 2 nozzle.

**4** For the ears, roll 2 green balls and shape into cones. Push a small blue ball into the wide end of each cone using a ball tool.

**5** Glue the ears to the head and add the eyes and nose. Add a thin curl of light blue fondant to make the hair.

CAKE DESIGN
For a really great effect, make a set of these monsters in all the colours of the rainbow and place each one on a cupcake with matching buttercream. In the design shown here, I have created a landscape based on rock and dry land. You can create this landscape on a board around a large cake or on the cake itself.

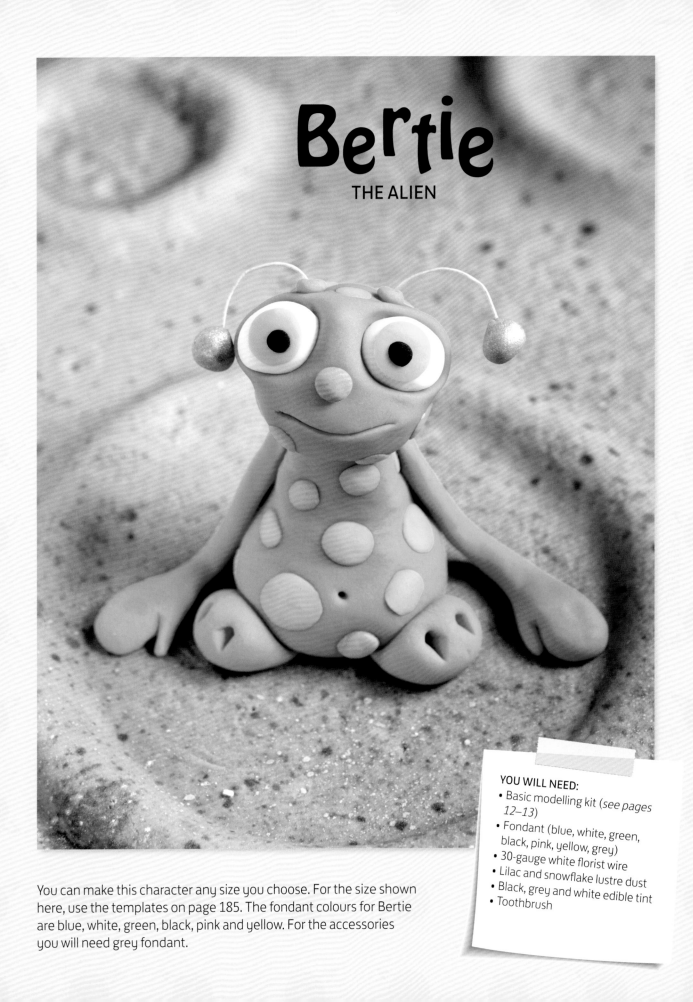

# Bertie

## THE ALIEN

You can make this character any size you choose. For the size shown here, use the templates on page 185. The fondant colours for Bertie are blue, white, green, black, pink and yellow. For the accessories you will need grey fondant.

**YOU WILL NEED:**
- Basic modelling kit (*see pages 12–13*)
- Fondant (*blue, white, green, black, pink, yellow, grey*)
- 30-gauge white florist wire
- Lilac and snowflake lustre dust
- Black, grey and white edible tint
- Toothbrush

1

Using blue fondant, roll a large ball for the body and a smaller one for the head.

2

Roll the larger ball into a cone shape. Use your thumb to press down on the front to make a big round tummy.

3

Add a belly button using a pin tool or cocktail stick.

4

To make a tail, roll a blue ball into a long cone shape and press the fatter end to flatten it.

5

Glue the flat section of the tail underneath the bottom. Push 1 or 2 lengths of spaghetti into the body, right to the base.

6

Shape the head ball into an oval and push it onto the body so the spaghetti is completely covered.

7

Use a large ball tool to make eye sockets. Create a thin rim around each eye by pressing the fondant against your finger with the ball tool.

8

Cut a groove into the fondant using a scalpel, to make a gently smiling mouth.

9

For the eyes, roll 2 white balls and cut in half. Use your fingertips to soften the cut sides. The eyes should be slightly oval.

TOP TIP
When making large eyes, always roll a ball or an oval and cut it in half. Only use the front half of the ball, otherwise the eyes will protrude too much. If this does occur, slice a little off the back and reshape.

10

Roll out some green fondant and cut out 2 circles (smaller than the white pieces). Glue them onto the white fondant (*see Top Tip, left*).

11

Make a small indent in each green circle and glue on 2 tiny black balls to make pupils.

12

Glue the completed eyes into the sockets.

13

Roll a small ball of pink fondant to make a nose.

14

Using yellow fondant, roll some small balls and press them onto the body so they are flat. Use your flat-ended colour shaper to smooth out the edges and hide the joins.

**TOP TIP**
When adding fondant spots, roll or press them so they are very thin before applying them to the body. Use a flat-ended colour shaper to blend the joins so the spots appear seamless.

15

Glue 2 tiny blue balls to the top of the head, ready to insert the antennae.

16

To make the feet, roll 2 blue balls. Using the side of your thumb, press 1 half of each ball to flatten.

17

Insert the angle chisel colour shaper into the front of each foot as shown, to create claws.

18

Attach the feet by applying glue to the flattened surface of each foot and positioning underneath the body.

**TOP TIP**
When making aliens, try to exaggerate some of their features by making them unusually large. Here I have given Bertie extra long arms and big eyes. This helps to make him look particularly alien-like, and not like any other character.

19

For the arms, roll 2 blue balls. Take 1 ball and shape into a sausage (longer than the body) with a ball at one end. Press the ball flat.

20

The flattened ball will be the hand. Cut out a piece of fondant to make a thumb, then shorten the thumb.

21

Using your thumb and finger, soften the edges of the thumb and the rest of the hand.

Repeat steps 19–21 to make the other arm, then glue both arms in place.

At this point, your alien should look like this.

To make the antennae, push a small ball of fondant onto a piece of 30-gauge florist wire (this is very easy to bend).

**TOP TIP**
Don't use wire if you're making a children's cake, as it isn't edible. If you want the alien to be fully edible, replace the wire with candy laces, rice noodles or anything edible and bendy.

Cover the balls in lilac and snowflake lustre dust.

Dip the ends of the wire in edible glue, then push them into the head, through the small balls you attached in step 24.

Your finished alien should look like this.

**TOP TIP**
Remember the key rule: the bigger the eyes, the cuter the character – this doesn't only apply to babies. Big eyes are perceived as cute all around the world.

## Planet

Roll some sausages of fondant and place them in a circle on the top of a cake or cake board to make a crater.

Roll out some grey fondant and lay it over the entire cake or board.

Make dents in the fondant using your ball tool.

Make edible paint in black, grey and white (*see page 9*). With a toothbrush, flick the paint over the fondant using black, then grey, then a little white.

**TOP TIP**
When flicking colour with a toothbrush, always make sure your table, wall and floor are well covered in case you flick paint in the wrong direction.

**CAKE DESIGN**
An alien that looks cute and vulnerable is best left as a solitary figure on a cake. For the picture opposite, I used a round cake, 30 cm in diameter, with a large surface area to make Bertie look a little lost and lonely on his own planet.

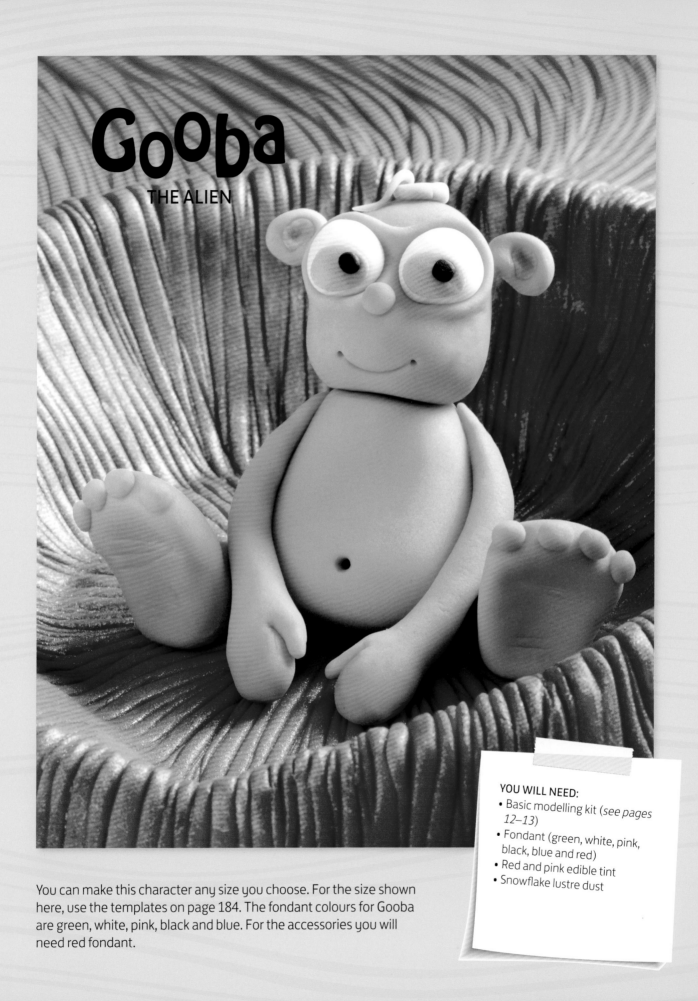

# GoOba

## THE ALIEN

You can make this character any size you choose. For the size shown here, use the templates on page 184. The fondant colours for Gooba are green, white, pink, black and blue. For the accessories you will need red fondant.

**YOU WILL NEED:**
- Basic modelling kit (*see pages 12–13*)
- Fondant (green, white, pink, black, blue and red)
- Red and pink edible tint
- Snowflake lustre dust

1

Roll a large green ball for the body and a smaller one for the head.

2

Take the larger ball and roll it into a cone shape.

3

Insert a piece of spaghetti into the body, right to the base, and make a belly button using a pin tool.

TOP TIP
A novelty character is almost always made more cute by the addition of a belly button.

4

Roll the smaller ball into an egg shape to make the head.

5

Place the head on the body, so that the spaghetti is completely covered.

6

Make eye sockets using a ball tool. To make a rim around each eye, use the tool to press the fondant against your finger. Ensure the sockets are the same shape.

7

Make a defined brow using a flat-ended colour shaper.

8

Use a size 2 nozzle to make a mouth.

9

Define the ends of the mouth by adding dimples with a pin tool.

10

Roll 2 balls of white fondant and cut them in half so they each have a flat base.

11

Glue the eyes into the sockets.

12

Roll out some pink fondant and cut out 2 small circles. Glue them onto the eyes and add 2 tiny black balls to make the pupils.

TOP TIP
To further exaggerate the cuteness of big eyes, make them look up towards the recipient of the cake, rather than facing forward.

13

At this stage, your alien should look like this.

14

Roll a green cone and bend the pointed end. Make an indent in the round end with a ball tool.

15

Fill the indent with a small ball of blue fondant, then glue in place and press flat.

16

Repeat steps 14–15 to make the second ear, then glue both ears in place.

17

Your alien should look like this.

18

Roll a sausage of blue fondant and twist into a curl.

19

Glue the curl on top of the head.

20

To make the feet, roll 2 balls of green fondant. Take 1 ball and form into a long cone shape, leaving a large part of the ball at one end.

21

Pinch the ball to make a flat foot shape. Make the foot as large as you can without making it too thin.

22

At the end of the foot, make 4 indents with a small ball tool to form toes.

23

Glue a tiny green ball into each indent – the balls should decrease slightly in size as you work along the foot.

**24** Cut off the pointed end of the leg so it isn't too long.

**25** Make slight creases in the foot using a scalpel.

**26** Repeat steps 20–25 to make the second leg, then attach both legs to the body using edible glue.

**27** Your alien should now look like this.

**28** To make the arms, roll 2 green balls into long sausages with a ball shape at one end.

**29** Take 1 arm and press the ball end to flatten, – this will make the hand. With a scalpel, cut a piece out of the hand to make a thumb.

**30** Use your finger and thumb to soften the edges of the thumb and the hand.

Gently push the thumb towards the hand.

**32** Repeat steps 29–31 to make the other arm. Attach the arms to the body using edible glue.

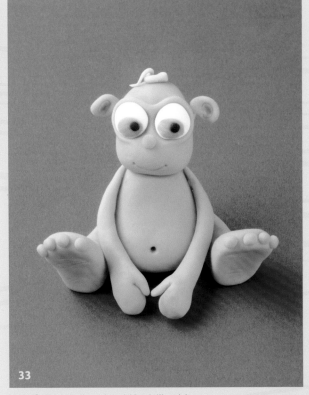

**33** Your finished alien should look like this.

## Eugene the alien

**1**

**2**

**3**

For Gooba's friend, make the body, 2 feet and arms as shown. Use the techniques applied to Gooba on pages 107–9.

Make the head as you made Gooba's head.

Attach the head to the body and glue in place.

## Radar the alien

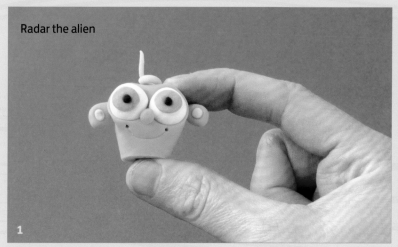

**1**

Make the head using the principles applied to Gooba, but give Radar a slightly longer head. Attach to the back of a crater on the cake or board. The hands are made in the same way as for Gooba (*see steps 29–31*).

## Landscape

**1**

Cover your cake or board with a ring of fondant, making it higher at the back than at the front.

**2**

**3**

Brush your cake or board with cooled boiled water and cover in red fondant. Using a wheel tool, draw lines over the fondant as shown.

To make paint, mix red, pink and white dusts with dipping solution (*see page 9*). Paint the fondant with streaks of colour to add texture.

**CAKE DESIGN**
In the image shown opposite, I have used a cake board to display Gooba and his friends. This line design would work perfectly on a tall cake or small cupcakes. Ensure you allow the lines to follow the natural shape of the cake.

# TROPICAL CREATURES

# ROXY
## THE OCTOPUS

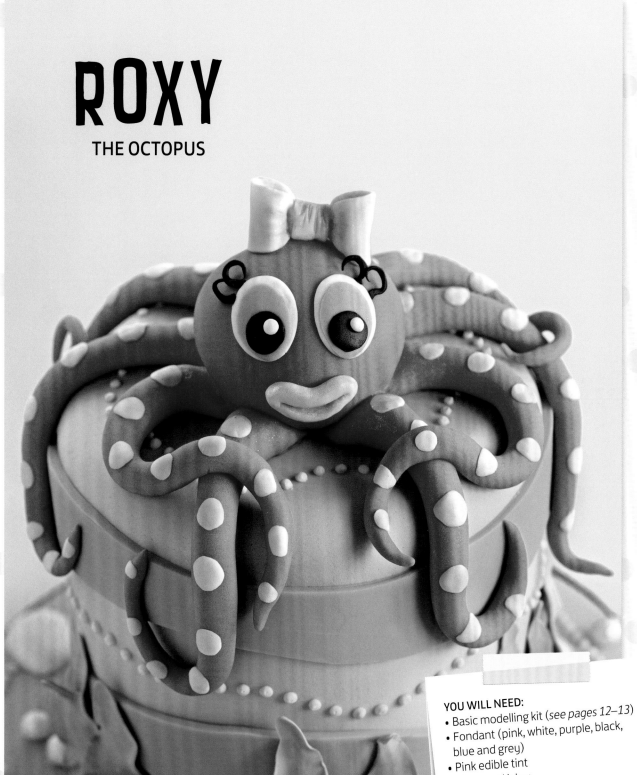

You can make this character any size you choose. For the size shown here, use the templates on page 186. The fondant colours for Roxy are pink, white, purple and black. For the accessories you will need blue, grey, pink, white and black fondant and green florist paste.

**YOU WILL NEED:**
- Basic modelling kit (*see pages 12–13*)
- Fondant (pink, white, purple, black, blue and grey)
- Pink edible tint
- Blue royal icing
- Piping bag
- Grey and snowflake lustre dust
- Shell moulds
- Lime green florist paste
- Leaf cutter
- Foam mat

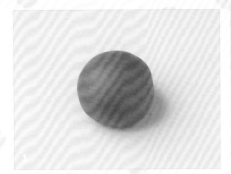

Roll a large ball of pink fondant for the body.

Cut out 2 white ovals using a cutter about 2 cm in length and 2 purple ovals with a cutter about 1.5 cm in length.

To make the eyes, glue the ovals onto the body as shown, and use a flat-ended colour shaper to create a seamless join.

Cut out 2 black fondant circles half the size of the purple ovals, and glue on tiny white fondant balls.

Glue the black circles in place as shown.

To make the mouth, roll a pink fondant sausage and bend it slightly. Push the wide end of a size 2 nozzle into the fondant to make a smile.

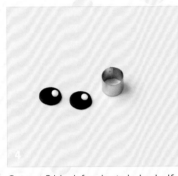

Glue the mouth in place, then dust the smile with pink edible tint.

To make the eyelashes, roll 4 balls of black fondant into cones, then curl as shown.

Glue 2 eyelashes above each eye.

**TOP TIP**
If you have a character that needs to be assembled on the cake, ensure you plan ahead and ice your cake at least one day before you want to add the character. Otherwise, the fondant on the cake will be too soft and will dent when touched.

To make the bow, cut 2 pieces of fondant into lozenge shapes. Fold over each piece and glue the ends together.

If you accidentally squash the bow, reopen using a ball tool.

Cut off the tip of each piece using a scalpel, then glue the 2 halves of the bow together.

Cut out a strip of fondant and wrap it around the join. Cut to size and glue the end underneath the bow.

Glue the bow onto the head and dust lightly with pink edible tint. (If you want to dust in the creases of the bow, do this before attaching it to the head.)

**15** Roxy needs to be assembled on the cake; cover your cake with light blue fondant now. Cut long wavy strips in dark blue fondant and glue around the sides.

**16** Using a pin tool, scratch lines onto the cake – these will guide you as you pipe the dots in the next step.

Put some blue royal icing into a piping bag and pipe dots along the scratched lines.

**18** Stop after every 15–20 dots and, using a damp brush, gently push down any peaks on your dots so they are all nicely rounded.

To make each leg, roll a ball of fondant into a cone about 15 cm long. Make a dent in the wider end with your thumb.

**20** Cover the leg with light pink balls, squashing them flat as you glue them on.

**TOP TIP**
Children don't mind if you use unrealistic colours, so have fun playing with your colour palette. As long as you give the character key features – like 8 legs for an octopus – your character will be recognisable.

**21** Curl the leg into a twisted shape.

Glue the leg onto the cake. (To ensure all the legs are the same distance from the middle, mark the centre with a dot of paste.)

Make another 7 legs and glue them in place around the centre dot. You can then glue on the body, or, if you want it to sit higher, add a ring of fondant as shown.

Your finished octopus should look like this.

## Benji the Clam

Roll a ball of light grey fondant about 4 cm in diameter.

Cut the ball in half.

Pinch the edges of the cut side of each half, to make them soft and wavy.

With a small ball tool make 2 indents for eyes, then gently mark both halves of the fondant all over the surface to make a shell pattern.

To make a tongue, cut out a pink semi-circle and mark a crease down the middle. Glue in place as shown.

**TOP TIP**
Whenever you are piping with royal icing, always have a small brush and a bowl of water to hand. Even the best pipers will occasionally have little peaks in their piping. These can be smoothed out by tapping them gently with a damp brush.

Glue the 2 halves of the clam together along 1 side. (If the mouth won't stay open, place a piece of fondant at the back of the tongue). Glue a length of white fondant around the mouth.

Glue on 2 white fondant balls for eyes, then add smaller black fondant pupils. Dust the clam with grey and snowflake lustre dust.

### Pearls and shells

TOP TIP
When using a mould, make sure no fondant or paste is hanging over the edge of the mould before removing the fondant.

Using a variety of shell moulds and white fondant or florist paste, make a selection of shell shapes (*see Top Tip, right*).

Dust the shells with snowflake lustre dust. To make pearls, roll fondant balls through the dust. Decorate the cake with shells and pearls.

### Seaweed

To make the seaweed, colour some florist paste in lime green and cut out some long leaf shapes.

On a foam mat, press the edges of the leaf with a ball tool to give a wave effect, then glue in place on the sides of the cake.

CAKE DESIGN
When making an octopus, whether on a large cake or a cupcake, it is usually best to assemble the character on the cake as you go along. Therefore, ensure you have prepared the size of your cake to fit your octopus. Here, I used a cake about 15 cm in diameter and 18 cm in depth. For cupcakes, make the cakes first and assemble the octopuses on the top so the legs can hang off the side.

# BOOMER

## THE FISH

YOU WILL NEED:
- Basic modelling kit (*see pages 12–13*)
- Fondant (yellow, white, blue, black and red)
- Red, orange and yellow edible tint
- Black edible ink pen
- Dark modelling chocolate
- 18-gauge florist wire
- Cotton
- Black florist paste

You can make this character any size you choose. For the size shown here, use the templates on page 187. The fondant colours for the fish are yellow, white, blue and black. For the accessories you will need red, blue and white fondant, brown modelling chocolate and black florist paste.

1

Roll a large ball of yellow fondant for the body.

2

Roll the ball into a cone shape.

3

To create a ridge along the centre of the cone, pinch the fondant between your index fingers.

4

Cut out a white fondant shape with an oval cutter 4 cm long. Remove a section to make a crescent.

5

Glue the crescent onto the yellow fondant as shown, for the teeth.

6

Push a ball tool into the fondant, pressing against your finger to create eye sockets.

7

Use a wheel tool to draw on the teeth as shown.

8

Roll a length of yellow fondant, then cut it in half.

9

Glue 1 half around the top of the mouth and the other around the bottom.

10

Where the 2 pieces meet, smooth out the seam using a pointed colour shaper.

11

To make the eyes, roll a 1 cm ball of white fondant and cut in half.

12

Pinch around the edge of each half so they each have a round top and a flat base.

13

Glue the eyes in position in the sockets (rounded sides facing up).

14

Roll out some light blue fondant, cut out 2 small circles, then glue them onto the white eyes.

**15**

Glue 2 small black fondant pupils onto the blue circles.

**16**

To make the eyelids, cut out 2 yellow circles, then cut out a crescent shape from each circle as shown.

**17**

Glue the crescent shapes around the eyes, tucking in the points at the sides.

**18**

Gently press a flat-ended colour shaper around each eyelid, about 1 mm from the back edge, to create a rim.

**19**

For the top fin, roll a sausage of yellow fondant and flatten into a harp shape. As you press the fondant between your fingers, the edges will become wavy.

**20**

For the tail fin, pinch a ball into a teardrop shape with wavy edges.

Draw lines over the surfaces of both fins using a wheel tool. Go over the same area several times so that the edges tear a little.

**22**

Add a line of glue along the ridge created in step 3, then glue on the top fin.

**23**

Secure the fin in place by pinching with your fingertips.

**24**

Glue on the tail fin in the same way.

**25**

To make the side fins, roll 2 balls of yellow fondant and press flat to create teardrop shapes.

**26**

Roll over both sides of each piece with a wheel tool, again allowing the fondant to tear at the edges.

**27**

Take 1 of the fins and glue the tip in place at the side of the fish.

**28**

Bend the fin around a brush or thin stick and glue the other end to the fish as shown.

**TOP TIP**

When you are making an animal that isn't particularly attractive, such as a fish or a turtle, aim to make it cute and cheeky so the recipient finds it hard to resist. Big eyes always make a character look very cute.

**29**

Take the second fin and glue the tip in place on the other side of the fish. Let it flap out to the side.

**30**

Mark the entire body with scales, using a smile tool as shown. Work from the face back to the tail.

**31**

Using red, orange and yellow edible tints, dust over the body.

**32**

Dust the fin along the base with slightly darker red and orange tints.

**TOP TIP**

For certain characters you may wish to have a blended colour. You can do this using edible tints. Here, rather than make the fish orange, I have used yellow and then dusted in reds, oranges and yellows. This gives a more realistic and interesting look to the fish.

**33**

Your finished fish should look like this.

Tropical Creatures **123**

## Willie the Worm

**1** Roll a ball of pale red fondant and shape it into a sausage. Turn up one end to create a head.

**2** Mark lines along the back of the worm using a scalpel.

**3** Draw on a face with black edible ink, and, if you wish, add little sausage shapes to some of the worms to make arms.

## Fishing rod

**1** Roll a thin sausage of dark modelling chocolate and insert a length of 18-gauge wire. (To make the rod edible, use spaghetti rather than wire and make the sausage thicker.)

**2** As you push in the wire the chocolate will bunch up, so roll out the chocolate with the wire inside on a board.

**3** Wrap some cotton around the end of the chocolate.

**4** Make a small hook from black florist paste, then twist the cotton onto the hook. Allow the hook to dry, then glue a worm in place and add arms.

## Waves

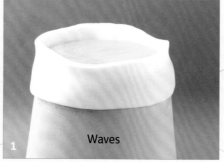

**1** Cover your cake with blue fondant. Glue a wavy strip of white fondant around the cake, letting it sit higher than the top of the cake.

**2** Add a layer of glue around the base of, and underneath, the first strip.

**3** Place another fondant strip over the glue. You can use a second white piece, or, for a smaller cake, start grading into light blue.

**4** Continue to add more strips in the same way, until you reach the base. Make each strip a little darker than the last, by adding colour to the fondant.

**CAKE DESIGN**
As a fish has no limbs, you need to consider how he will fit into your design. Here, I made a tall cake using two 15 cm cakes and one 10 cm cake. I cut, levelled and stacked the cakes, then carved them to make the sloped sides. I then covered the cakes. The 'Waves' technique can also be used for grass, sand and fire.

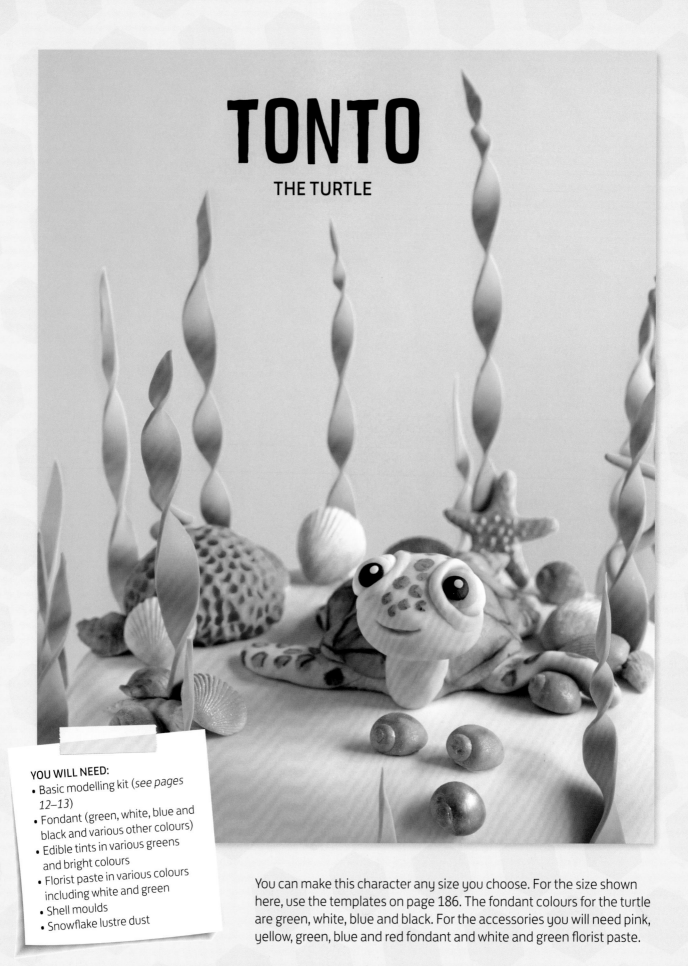

# TONTO

## THE TURTLE

**YOU WILL NEED:**
- Basic modelling kit (*see pages 12–13*)
- Fondant (green, white, blue and black and various other colours)
- Edible tints in various greens and bright colours
- Florist paste in various colours including white and green
- Shell moulds
- Snowflake lustre dust

You can make this character any size you choose. For the size shown here, use the templates on page 186. The fondant colours for the turtle are green, white, blue and black. For the accessories you will need pink, yellow, green, blue and red fondant and white and green florist paste.

1. Roll out some light green fondant about 3 mm thick, and cut out an oval about 7 cm long.

2. Roll out some darker green fondant about 10 mm thick, and cut out an oval the same size as in step 1.

3. Glue the darker green oval onto the lighter one.

4. Use your fingers to curve the edges of the fondant – like a shell. It doesn't need to be perfect as it won't be seen.

5. To make the back flippers, roll 2 light green fondant balls and pinch them flat, curving them slightly at the ends.

6. To make the front flippers, pinch 2 light green balls into long flat cones.

7. Using a scalpel, make 4 cuts in the dark green oval, ready to insert the flippers.

8. Put some glue into each of the holes.

9. Put the flippers into the holes. Twist 1 front flipper up, so you can slip a small shell underneath it later.

**TOP TIP**
When you make a turtle, try to make one flipper twisted to give the illusion of movement.

10. Roll out some more dark green fondant and cut out a larger oval (about 8 cm long).

11. Rest the oval over the body. If it's too small, gently pull it to stretch it a little.

12. Glue the fondant onto the body to create the shell. It should be wrapped around the arms so they appear to be pushing out from underneath.

**13**

Cut out a section at the front of the body using a round cutter. This is where the neck will go.

**14**

Using a wheel tool, draw hexagon shapes all over the shell (they don't need to be perfect).

**15**

Draw a line around the edge of the shell, about 3 mm up from the base.

**16**

Dust the shell with edible tints in different shades of green. Apply randomly for a more realistic look.

**17**

Mix the darkest green tint that you've used with dipping solution, and, using a size 1 brush, paint in the hexagon lines.

**18**

Paint light green spots on the arms and legs.

**19**

Outline the spots in a darker green.

**TOP TIP**
A turtle's neck should always appear as if it is stretching out of the shell. This is a key characteristic of a turtle.

**20**

At this stage, your turtle should look like this. Make sure the flippers are now secure.

**21**

To make the neck, roll a ball of light green fondant into a cone.

**22**

Glue the neck into the space you cut out of the body, then insert 2 lengths of spaghetti as shown.

**23**

Roll a ball of light green fondant for the head.

**24**

To make the eye sockets, push a large ball tool into the fondant and press it against your finger.

**25**

To make rims around the eye sockets, gently push around the eye line with a flat-ended colour shaper as shown.

**26** Paint the head with spots in the same way as you did the arms and legs, then make a smile using a size 2 nozzle.

**27** Push the head onto the pieces of spaghetti and glue in place.

**28** To make the eyes, cut a 1 cm ball of white fondant into 2 halves.

**29** Pinch around the flat side of each semi-circle to define the edges.

**30** Glue 2 blue fondant circles to the whites of the eyes, then glue on 2 black circles and, finally, tiny white pupils.

**31** Glue the eyes into the sockets to complete your turtle. Your finished turtle should look like this.

**Shells**

**1** Press florist paste (or a mixture of half florist paste and half fondant) into a shell mould. Ensure you can see the outlines, then remove.

**2** Make shells in pink, lemon yellow, light green and light blue.

**3** Dust the shells with edible tints, using a rainbow of colours.

Add snowflake lustre dust to the shells to make them shimmer.

Make green shells using a mixture of red and green tints, then add snowflake lustre dust. The red will disappear as it blends in.

You should now have a selection of shells in different colours and shapes.

Corals

To make sponges, roll balls of fondant in different colours. To achieve this pattern, push in a small ball tool all over the surface.

For the pattern shown above, roll a wheel tool all over the surface.

The pattern shown here is made by snipping the fondant with the tip of a pair of scissors.

### TOP TIP
When making abstract patterns on sea fauna, use household objects like a sponge, fabric, a fork or lace to create different effects.

Using any colour, roll a ball of fondant into a cone and push a large ball tool into the wider end. Make several of these corals to group together.

If you wish to pattern them further, use a wheel tool to draw lines around the rim.

Roll out some florist paste and make holes with a nozzle and a round cutter. Bend into shape and leave to dry for at least 2 hours.

Seaweed

Roll out some green florist paste and cut out long thin triangles. Hold each one at both ends and twist. Leave to dry for at least 24 hours and ideally 48 hours.

### CAKE DESIGN
For the picture opposite, I baked a round cake 18 cm in diameter and 10 cm in depth. The seaweed is pushed into the fondant on the cake and the corals. Any joins are covered by shells and fauna. Tropical marine life is very colourful so use lots of colour in the shells around the cake.

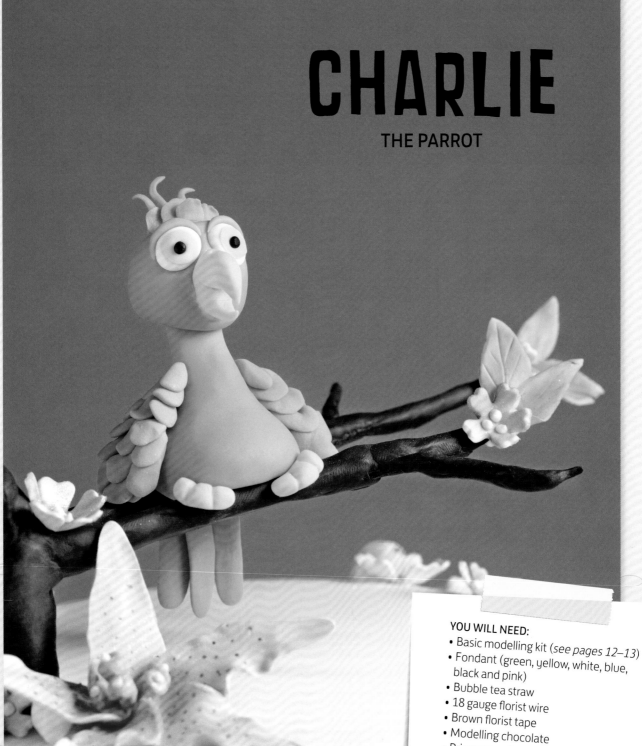

# CHARLIE

## THE PARROT

You can make this character any size you choose. For the size shown here, use the templates on page 187. The fondant colours for the parrot are green, yellow, white, blue and black. For the accessories you will need white, pink and light green fondant. You will also need white and green florist paste.

**YOU WILL NEED:**
- Basic modelling kit (*see pages 12–13*)
- Fondant (green, yellow, white, blue, black and pink)
- Bubble tea straw
- 18 gauge florist wire
- Brown florist tape
- Modelling chocolate
- Primrose cutter set
- White and green florist paste
- Purple lustre dust
- Snowflake, green, brown and cream edible tints
- Variety of large petal cutters
- White stamen

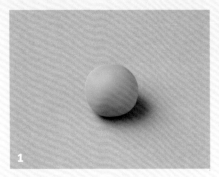

1

Roll a ball of light green fondant for the body.

2

Roll part of the ball into a neck shape as shown, keeping the rounded section at the base fairly large.

3

Push a length of spaghetti into the fondant, right to the base.

4

Pinch the fondant on one side so that you have a slightly pointed area to attach the tail feathers to.

5

To make the wings, roll 2 balls of green fondant and shape them into cones.

6

Take 1 cone and flatten it between your thumb and finger.

7

Glue the first wing in place as shown.

8

Repeat steps 6–7 to make the second wing.

9

Your parrot should now look like this.

10

To make the wing feathers, roll some small balls of darker green fondant and press each one flat.

11

Pinch the end of each piece to make feather shapes.

TOP TIP
Parrots look good in many different colours, but they are most effective if you stick to red, blue, yellow or green. The principles used for this parrot also apply to making a Toucan.

**12**

Cover the wings with the feathers, starting at the back and the bottom of each wing and overlapping the feathers.

**13**

Your parrot wings should look like this.

**14**

Next, your parrot needs a branch to sit on. Push a bubble tea straw into your cake and cut it to the height of the cake.

**15**

Group together 6–8 lengths of 18-gauge florist wire, then wrap with brown florist tape to about 3 cm higher than the cake.

**16**

Insert the wire into the straw, then bend to form a right angle about 3 cm above the cake height.

TOP TIP
For food-safety reasons, florist wire must never come into contact with your cake. If you are intending to put wire into your cake, either put a flower pick into the cake and sit the wire in the pick, or, as shown here, cover the wire with florist tape, then put it into a bubble tea straw (or other wide drinking straw).

**17**

Cut the wires using wire cutters, then bend them to make 2 main branches and a couple of twigs (do this by bending the tips of the wires).

Wrap brown florist tape around the wires as shown.

**19**

Cover the wires with modelling chocolate.

**20**

Smooth the chocolate between your thumb and finger. The tape underneath will give it a realistic bumpy effect.

**21**

Dip a pointed colour shaper in water and use it to smooth any remaining unwanted bumps in the chocolate.

Sit your parrot in the tree so that it perches between the branches. You can glue it in place if you wish.

To make the tail feathers, roll 3 long dark green cones and press flat.

Glue the tail feathers in place on the back of the parrot.

**TOP TIP**
If you would like your parrot's toes to grip on the branch, create deeper cuts in the yellow fondant and bend them around the branch.

To make the feet, using yellow fondant roll 2 crescent shapes and mark 2 lines on each one with a stitching tool.

Glue the feet to the branch at the front of the parrot's body.

To make the head, roll a ball of green fondant and make it slightly egg shaped (not too pointed).

Make 2 indents with a ball tool for the eye sockets, then cut out an oval piece to make a hole for the beak to slot into.

Make some head feathers by rolling little cones of green fondant and using any spare wing feathers.

For the eyes, roll a ball of white fondant and cut it in half.

Smooth down the 2 halves so they are round on top and flat underneath.

Glue a circle of light blue fondant to each eye, then make an indent in each one, ready for the pupils.

**33** Roll 2 tiny balls of black fondant for the pupils and glue them into the indents, then glue the eyes into the sockets.

**34** To make the eye lids, roll 2 thin green sausages and bend into arches. Glue in place to cover the tops of the eyes.

**35** Glue the head onto the body.

**36** Make sure you are happy with the direction in which the head is facing.

**37** To make the beak, roll a ball of yellow fondant and gently flatten it. Make a line as shown. (*See Top Tip, right.*)

TOP TIP
The beak is tricky to get right first time. Always measure the ball of yellow fondant against the face to make sure it isn't going to be too big or too small.

**38** Cut out a section to make a mouth.

**39** Cut away the back of the fondant with a round cutter.

**40** Make 2 nostrils on the top using a pin tool.

TOP TIP
Allow the beak to harden a little before gluing it in place. This way, you won't squash it if you press too hard.

**41** Glue the beak into the hollow made in step 28 (*see Top Tip, left*).

**42** Check that the beak looks correct from the side.

**TOP TIP**
You don't have to balance your parrot on a branch. If he is on the cake instead, just flip his tail feathers out so they are horizontal rather than vertical. If you are placing him on the tree, place him between 2 branches. By putting his feet on the front branch only, it will look like he is balancing on that branch.

Also check that the beak doesn't look too big from the front. Your finished parrot should look like this.

**Small flowers**

To make the flowers, roll out some white florist paste and cut out some small petals. Leave to dry in a foam flower tray – they will naturally curl. Paint with purple lustre dust and snowflake tint.

**Leaves**

To make the leaves, roll out some light green florist paste and cut out leaf shapes in various sizes. Cut out triangular pieces from along the edges as shown, then mark on veins with a wheel tool.

Bend the leaves and allow to dry for at least 2 hours and ideally 24 hours, then dust with green edible tint. You can also make tiny leaves to sit on the tree. Glue any leaves to the tree.

**Bamboo**

Roll a sausage of light green fondant about 8 mm wide, then cut into pieces of varying length. Push a large ball tool into both ends of each piece.

Dust the bamboo with a mixture of green, brown and cream edible tints.

**Larger flowers**

Choose any petal cutter and cut out 5 or 6 petals from florist paste.

Use a ball tool to give the petals wavy edges.

Leave the petals to dry in a foam flower tray for at least 2 hours and ideally 24 hours.

Roll a ball of fondant and glue the petals around it as shown. (Some flowers require 5 petals and others 6 petals.)

Roll a ball of fondant and push in the stamen. (These are not edible so leave them out if you prefer.)

Glue the flower centre into the middle of the flower.

CAKE DESIGN
For the design opposite, I used a round cake 20 cm in diameter and 12 cm in depth and covered it in cream fondant. I placed the bamboo around the sides and decorated the branches and the cake with tropical-looking flowers.

# Farm Animals

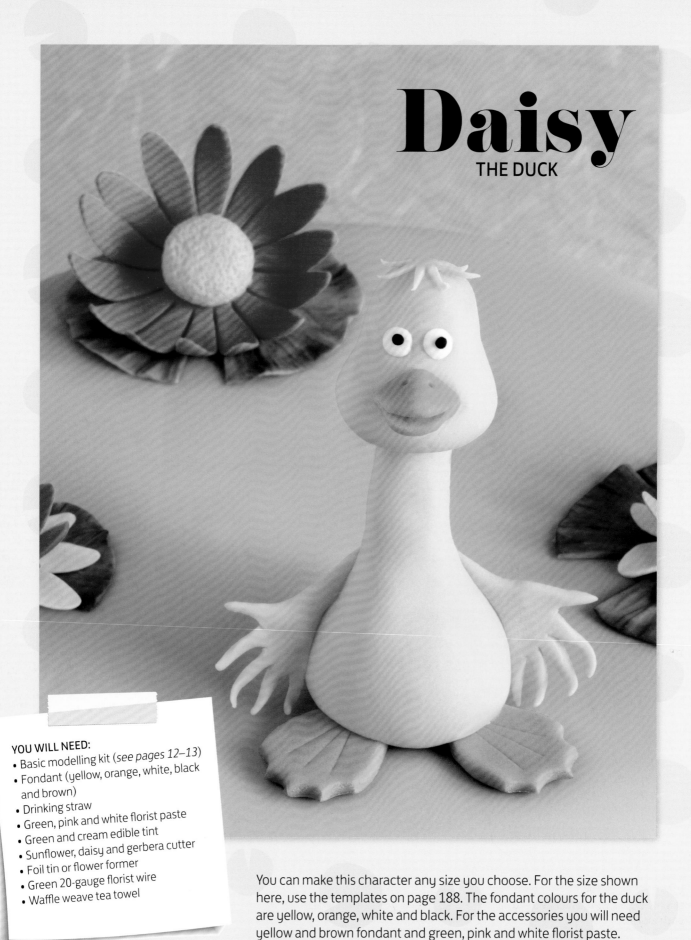

# Daisy
## THE DUCK

You can make this character any size you choose. For the size shown here, use the templates on page 188. The fondant colours for the duck are yellow, orange, white and black. For the accessories you will need yellow and brown fondant and green, pink and white florist paste.

1

Roll 2 balls of yellow fondant for the body and the head.

2

Shape the larger ball into a cone. Lengthen the pointed end to make the neck, and keep the wider end rounded to make a big bottom.

3

Push a length of spaghetti (or 2 if needed) downwards into the fondant to make a support as shown.

4

Using your thumb and finger, pinch the bottom to form a more pointed tail.

5

Take the smaller ball and roll one end in the palm of your hand to make the top of the head.

TOP TIP
To make your characters appear friendly and cute, always make the 'brain' end of the head smaller than the mouth end.

6

The head should be shaped as shown here.

7

Position the head on top of the neck (do not glue).

8

Roll out some orange fondant and use a 1.5 cm tear cutter to cut out 2 shapes. These will make the feet.

9

Using the end of a drinking straw, cut out semi-circles along the rounded end of each foot.

10

Using the back of a scalpel, mark 3 lines along each foot to indicate webbing.

11

Cut off the pointed end of each foot.

**12**

Glue the feet in place underneath the body of the duck.

**13**

To make the arms, roll 2 balls of yellow fondant. Roll one end of each ball into a thin sausage.

**14**

Take 1 wing and flatten the ball-shaped end with your fingertip.

**15**

Using a scalpel, cut 4 long thin triangles out of the flattened end to make 5 fingers.

**16**

Gently pinch each finger to make a soft curved shape.

**17**

Repeat steps 14–16 to make the other arm, then glue both arms to the body (it's easiest if you remove the head first).

**18**

To make the hair, roll out a piece of yellow fondant very thinly.

**19**

Cut out a small irregular star shape with 6 or 7 points.

**20**

Glue the star shape onto the head to make the hair, then attach with edible glue.

**21**

Turn up the ends of the hair using your fingertip.

**22**

To make the beak, roll a ball of orange fondant into a cone shape.

**23**

Hold the beak between your fingertips and cut a slit in the round end to make the mouth.

24

Cut off the point of the cone.

25

Add 2 nostrils using a pin tool.

26

Glue the beak in position, making sure it's two thirds of the way down the face, covering both the mouth and the nose area.

27

For the eyes, roll 2 white balls of fondant and glue in place, then add 2 tiny balls of black fondant to make the pupils.

**TOP TIP**
To make hair for animals, roll some fondant very thinly and cut out a star shape. Then turn up the points using your fingertips or a cocktail stick.

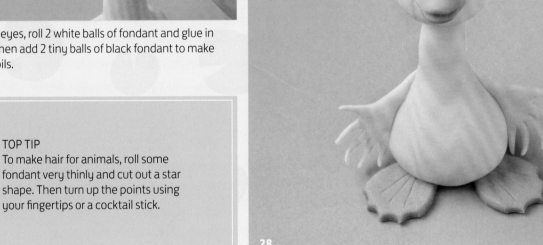

28

Your finished duck should look like this.

**Ducklings**

1

Roll 2 small balls of yellow fondant to make a body and a head. Glue the smaller ball on top of the larger one.

2

To make the feet, repeat the method used for the duck (steps 8–11) but use a smaller cutter. For the wings, squash 2 yellow balls into flat wing shapes.

3

Glue the wings and feet in place.

**4**

To make a tiny beak, roll a small orange ball and shape the tip into a point using your thumb and fingertips as shown.

**5**

Add little black fondant eyes to complete your duckling, or, alternatively, use black non-pareils. Repeat steps 1–5 to make more ducklings.

**1** Lily pad

Cut out a circle of green florist paste or fondant, and cut out a section as shown.

**2**

Roll a veining tool over the surface to create a lily pad texture.

**3**

Dust the edges of the lily pad with dark green edible tint.

Pink flowers

**1**

Roll out some pink and white florist paste and cut out flower shapes using a sunflower, daisy and gerbera cutter.

**2**

Leave to dry in a foil tin or flower former for at least 2 hours and ideally 24 hours.

**3**

Roll a ball of yellow fondant for each flower and prick them all over with a pin tool.

**4**

Glue each yellow ball into the centre of a flower.

Rushes and reeds

**1**

Cut lengths of florist wire and dip in glue. Push each one into a brown fondant sausage and roll over a waffle weave tea towel to emboss. Dust with light cream or buttermilk

**2**

For reeds, cut long thin triangles of green florist paste and curl the tips. Leave to dry for 24 hours.

CAKE DESIGN
For the design opposite, I have used a cake of approximately 20 cm in diameter and 12 cm in depth. The cake is covered in blue fondant and the flowers are added to the top with scattered ducklings. The sides of the cake are decorated with reeds and rushes. You could also paint water ripples onto the blue fondant using paste food colouring mixed with water.

# Coco

## THE COW

**YOU WILL NEED:**
- Basic modelling kit (*see pages 12–13*)
- Fondant (white, black, pink and green)
- Small heart plunger cutter
- Small blossom plunger cutter
- Acetate smoother

You can make this character any size you choose. For the size shown here, use the templates on page 189. The fondant colours for Coco are white, black, pink and green. You will need the same colours for the accessories.

1. Roll 2 balls of white fondant for the body and the head.

2. Roll the larger ball into a wide-based cone shape.

3. Push a length of spaghetti downwards into the fondant to make a support as shown.

4. Roll the smaller ball into an egg shape.

5. Position the head on the spaghetti to check that the head is in proportion with the body.

6. To make the patch on the body, roll a ball of black fondant and press flat. Pinch the edges to make an irregular shape.

7. Glue the patch onto the body and soften the edges using a flat-ended colour shaper.

8. Roll out some light pink fondant and cut an oval shape about the same size as the wider end of the head.

9. Gently pinch the edges flat.

10. Place the head on the body and glue the oval to the face. Flatten the edges using a flat-ended colour shaper, to make a seamless join.

11. Using the small end of a ball tool, make 2 indents for the nostrils.

TOP TIP
When working with black and white, make all the white parts together, then all the black parts. Black fondant will always leave a residue on your hands, so wash them before moving on to the next stage so you don't turn your white fondant grey.

**12**

Gently push the wide end of a size 2 nozzle into the pink fondant to make a smile.

**13**

Using a pin tool, make 2 holes for the eyes.

**14**

Above the eyes, make 2 larger holes for the horns.

**15**

For the horns, roll 2 small white cone shapes.

**16**

Glue the cones into the holes you made for the horns.

**17**

Roll 2 small balls of black fondant and glue them into the holes you made for the eyes. Press flat.

**18**

Open the mouth slightly by pushing the bottom lip down using a pin tool. It doesn't matter if the fondant cracks as it will be covered.

**19**

Roll out some green fondant and cut out a leaf shape using a small tear cutter. Make leaf vein markings with a scalpel.

**20**

Roll some green fondant to make grass, then glue the leaf and the grass into the mouth. Don't glue the head in place yet.

TOP TIP
With all characters, mark the position of key features such as eyes, ears and mouth using a pin tool. Do this early on so that you don't spoil your character at a later stage by gluing something in the wrong place.

**21**

Cut out 2 large white tear shapes and 2 smaller pink ones. Glue a pink tear onto a white one and press to flatten.

**22**

Take 1 tear shape and fold as shown, then gently bend back the open end to make an ear.

23

Cut off the pointed end using a scalpel. Repeat steps 22–3 to make the other ear.

24

Glue the ears in place just below the horns – they should be wide open. Add any additional black fondant patches to the body.

25

To make the legs, roll 2 balls of white fondant and shape into cones.

26

Using a small cutter, cut out 2 hearts from black fondant and glue one to the base of each foot. Trim the legs so they sit close to the body.

27

Glue the legs in place at the base of the body.

28

For the arms, roll 2 white balls into cone shapes. Bend each one in the middle to make elbows.

29

Cut out 2 black fondant hearts and glue them to the hands. Attach small patches of black fondant to the arms.

30

Attach the arms to the body using edible glue.

**TOP TIP**
Always focus on key characteristics. For example, elephants have big ears, cows and giraffes have floppy ears and cats have pointy ears. It's these features that will define the personality of your creation.

31

When all the parts are in place and you're happy that you have enough black patches, gently lift the head and glue it in position.

32

For the tail, roll a ball of white fondant into a long thin sausage and make 5 pointed cones from black fondant.

33

Hold the black pieces and pinch the ends together.

Glue the black piece to one end of the white tail and glue the other end to the back of the cow. Make a tiny flower to attach to her head.

TOP TIP
Always glue your characters to the cake when you have finished, and before you attempt to move it, to avoid them toppling off when you pick up the cake.

Your finished cow should look like this.

### Patches on the cake

Cover your cake in white fondant. Roll out some black fondant and cut out a random shape with a wavy edge.

Position the patch on the cake and smooth down using a piece of food-safe acetate. You don't need to use glue.

Place patches around the cake and put a pink (or blue) patch in the centre for the cow to sit on. Decorate with flowers and grass as shown.

CAKE DESIGN
Here, I used a cake about 16 cm in diameter and 15 cm in depth. The design of the cake was based on the pattern of the cow. I covered the cake in white fondant, then applied the larger black pieces. You could reverse the colours and make the cake black with white patches. Alternatively, you could use brown and white fondant.

# Barnaby

## THE SHEEP

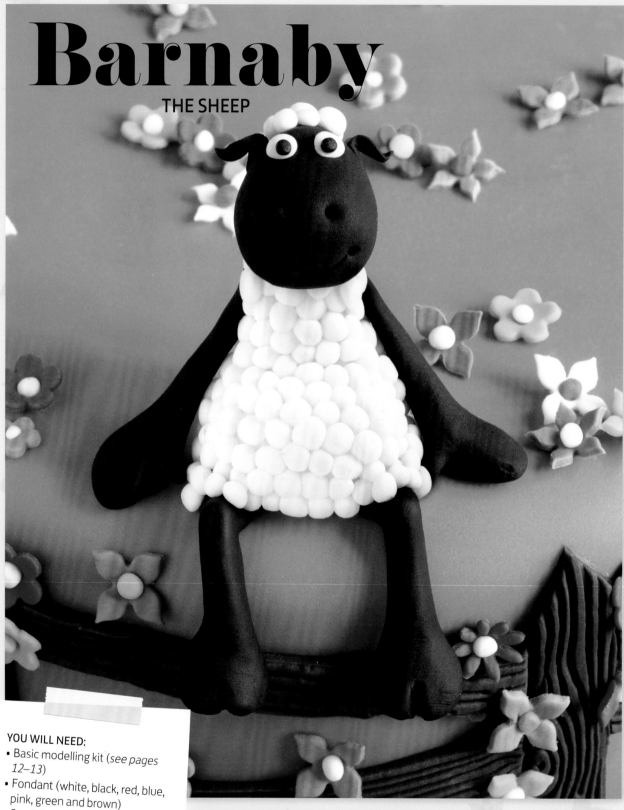

**YOU WILL NEED:**
- Basic modelling kit (*see pages 12–13*)
- Fondant (white, black, red, blue, pink, green and brown)
- Small flower cutters (blossom, jasmine and daisy)
- Bark embossing mat
- Green royal icing
- Piping bag with grass nozzle

You can make this character any size you choose. For the size shown here, use the templates on page 189. The fondant colours for Barnaby are white and black. For the accessories you will need red, black, white, blue, pink, green and brown fondant.

**1**

Roll a large white ball for the body and a smaller black ball for the head.

**2**

Roll the white ball into a cone shape, making sure the narrower end is quite thin.

**3**

Push a length of spaghetti downwards into the fondant to make a support as shown.

**4**

Roll lots of small white balls and glue them all over the body, starting at the base. (*See Top Tip on page 157.*)

**5**

Make sure the spaghetti is still visible when the body is completely covered.

**6**

Roll the black ball into an egg shape.

**7**

Position the head on the body – don't add glue at this stage.

**8**

Use a small ball tool to mark the holes for the eyes.

**9**

Make nostrils using a pin tool as shown.

**10**

Use the wide end of a size 2 nozzle to make a smile.

**11**

To make the eyes, roll 2 small balls of white fondant and glue them into the holes made in step 8.

**12**

Add 2 tiny balls of black fondant for the pupils.

**13**

Roll 5 or 6 small balls of white fondant and glue them to the top of the head.

**14**

Roll 2 black balls for the ears. Take 1 ball and press it flat between your thumb and finger. Bend it in the middle to make a right angle.

**15**

Repeat step 14 to make the other ear, then glue both ears in place, either side of the balls on the top of the head.

**16**

Your sheep should look like this.

**17**

To make the arms, roll 2 balls of black fondant into cone shapes.

**18**

Taking 1 of the arms, flatten the wider end to make a hand. Using a scalpel, cut out a small triangle to make a thumb.

**19**

Use the tip of your finger to soften the edges of the thumb and the hand. Repeat steps 18–19 to make the other arm.

**20**

Attach the arms to either side of the body using edible glue, then cover the joins with a few more white fondant balls.

**21**

To make the legs, roll 2 balls of black fondant into long cones.

**22**

Take 1 leg and pinch the wider end of the cone so that the base is flat. Cut a small groove into the front to create hooves.

**23**

Bend the leg in the middle to form a right angle, then press the narrow end to flatten. Repeat steps 22–3 to make the other leg.

**TOP TIP**
To create a more vulnerable and innocent looking sheep, gently turn the feet inwards rather than having the toes pointing forwards. Nervous characters tend to have their toes pointing inwards.

**24**

Glue the legs underneath the body. You will need to do this on the side of the cake so that the legs can dangle off the side.

25

Your finished sheep should look like this.

1

**Romeo the Reclining Sheep**

Romeo's body, head and legs are made in the same way as for Barnaby, but the legs are attached at a different angle using spaghetti or glue.

2

For Romeo's arms, follow steps 17–20, opposite, but bend them at the elbows as shown.

3

Romeo should now look like this.

**Poppy the Ladybird**

1

For the body, roll a ball of red fondant into a cone and cut off the narrow end using a scalpel.

2

Use a wheel tool to make a groove down the middle of the cone.

3

Roll some small black balls and glue them to the body, then press flat. Roll a small black ball for the head.

4

For the eyes, roll 2 small white balls and 2 tiny black balls. Use a size 2 nozzle to make a smile.

5

For the antennae, glue 2 small black cones onto the head. Bend them carefully.

**TOP TIP**
Don't be tempted to roll the balls to cover the sheep's body in advance, because they need to be soft in order to fit together and stick in place.

## Cedric the Snail

**1**
Using blue fondant, roll a sausage shape.

**2**
Bend the fondant about a third of the way along, to make a right angle.

**3**
Use a smile tool to create a mouth.

**4**
For the eyes, roll 2 blue balls and glue them to the face. Using a small ball tool, make an indent in each eye.

**5**
Roll 2 small white balls and push into the indents, then add 2 tiny black pupils.

**6**
To make the shell, roll a long sausage of darker blue fondant, then roll it up as shown.

**7**
Make lines along the shell using a wheel tool.

**8**
Glue the shell onto the snail's body as shown. Repeat the process in pink to make Winnie, Cedric's girlfriend.

## Flowers

**1**
Make flowers in various colours and shapes using a range of small flower cutters. You will need about 100 flowers for a 20 cm cake.

## Fence

**1**
Roll out some brown fondant and cover with a bark embossing mat. Put pressure on the mat to leave a pattern on the fondant.

**2**
Cut the fondant into strips of equal length. Make some of the strips pointed at one end, to form the vertical sections.

**3**
Glue the vertical strips in place, spacing them evenly around the cake, then add the horizontal strips.

**4**
To make the grass, pipe green royal icing or buttercream around the base of the cake using a piping bag with a grass nozzle.

### CAKE DESIGN
For the design opposite, I placed Barnaby and Romeo in a field of flowers. I used a cake about 20 cm in diameter and 10 cm in depth and covered it with green fondant. Fencing sits around the cake and flowers help to cover the joins. I used grass piping around the base to cover the join between the cake and the board.

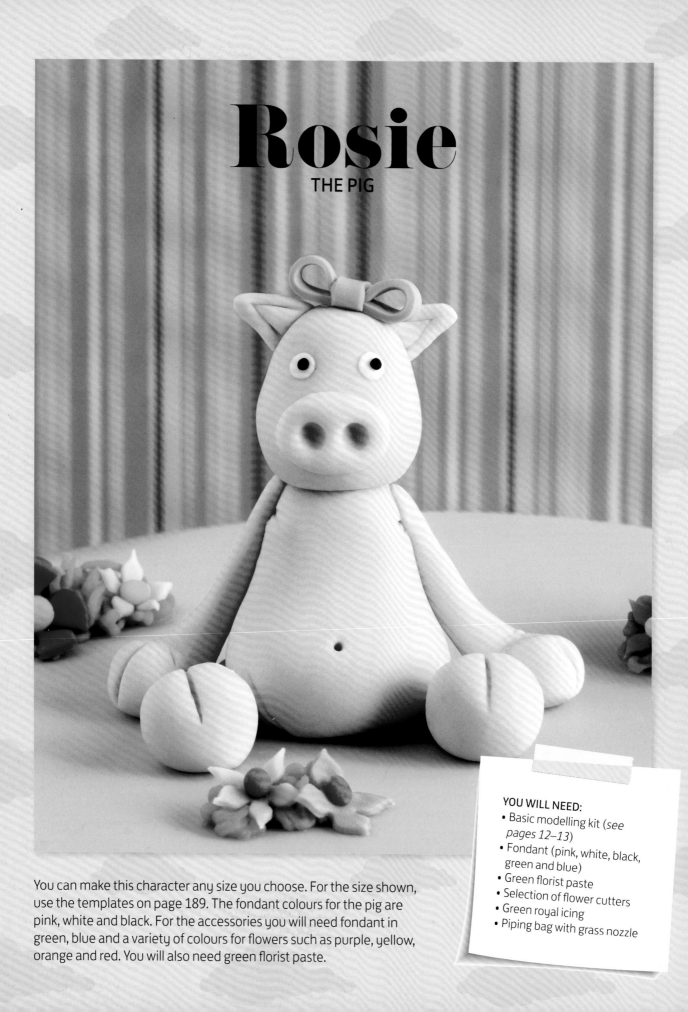

# Rosie
## THE PIG

You can make this character any size you choose. For the size shown, use the templates on page 189. The fondant colours for the pig are pink, white and black. For the accessories you will need fondant in green, blue and a variety of colours for flowers such as purple, yellow, orange and red. You will also need green florist paste.

**YOU WILL NEED:**
- Basic modelling kit (*see pages 12–13*)
- Fondant (pink, white, black, green and blue)
- Green florist paste
- Selection of flower cutters
- Green royal icing
- Piping bag with grass nozzle

**1** Roll 2 balls of pink fondant for the body and the head.

**2** Roll the large ball into a cone and press down in the middle, on one side, to make a tummy. Insert a piece of spaghetti. Make a belly button using a pin tool.

TOP TIP
To make a fondant pig, use a fairly pale pink. There is no other colour to break up a brighter shade and a soft pink gives a prettier finish.

**3** Roll the smaller ball into a rounded cone shape as shown.

TOP TIP
Try to avoid gluing 2 ball shapes together. Flattening the side of each ball that you want to attach will create a wider surface area for gluing. This will make your character more sturdy and less likely to come apart when being moved around.

**4** Position the head on the body to check the proportions (don't add glue at this stage).

**5** Using the back of a scalpel, make small creases for the folds in the skin underneath the arms (which will be added later).

**6** For the legs, roll 2 balls of pink fondant into long droplet shapes.

**7** Take 1 leg and, using a scalpel, make a groove in the wider end to mark the trotter. Repeat with the second leg.

**8** Glue the legs in position.

**9** To make the arms, roll 2 balls – smaller than those you used for the legs – and, again, shape them into long droplets but turn up the wider end a little.

**10** Take 1 arm and make a groove, using your scalpel, to mark the trotter. Repeat with the other arm.

**11**

Glue the arms in place, ensuring that the trotters are pointing forwards on the work surface.

**12**

Your pig should now look like this.

**13**

Roll out some pink fondant to a thickness of about 5 mm. Cut out an oval shape for the snout.

**14**

Glue the snout onto the face, covering the nose and mouth area.

**15**

To make the ears, roll 2 small balls of fondant and pinch one end with your thumb and finger to make a point.

**16**

Take 1 ear and cut off the rounded end, leaving a soft-edged triangle. Make a groove in the ear to show a fold.

**17**

Make a slot with a pin tool for the ear to fit into.

**18**

Repeat steps 16–17 to make the other ear, then glue both ears in place.

**19**

Use a small ball tool to make 2 indents for the nostrils. Ensure these are central.

**20**

Roll 2 small white fondant balls for the eyes and use a pin tool to mark their position on the face.

**21**

Glue the eyes in place and add 2 tiny black fondant balls for the pupils.

**22**

Roll out a piece of green florist paste and cut 2 strips about 4 mm wide.

**23** Take 1 strip and lightly fold over one end. Decide how big you want the loop to be, then mark the position on the fondant.

**24** Unfold the strip and use the mark you have made to work out how long the other end of the bow should be. Cut off the excess.

**25** Apply glue over the mark.

**26** Fold in the 2 ends of the strip so they sit on the mark.

**27** Use the other strip to cover the join by wrapping it around the centre of the bow. Glue in place, then trim off the ends.

**28** To make a curly tail, roll a thin sausage of pink fondant.

**29** Wind the tail around a paintbrush handle and leave to set for 10 minutes.

**30** Gently slide the tail off the brush and glue to the back of the pig.

**31** Your finished pig should look like this.

**Landscape**

Cover your cake board with green fondant and your cake with blue fondant. Place a wavy green strip around the sides of the cake to make hills. Roll a stitching tool around the edges of the hills.

Use a selection of flower cutters to make a variety of flowers and glue them onto the green fondant. Cut long green triangles to make the stems and glue them in place.

Use a pin tool to make a line of dots around the flowers, replicating the effect of the stitching tool. For large straight areas, use the stitching tool.

Pipe green royal icing or buttercream around the base of the cake with a grass nozzle, to cover the join between the cake and the board. Decorate with flowers and grass as desired.

CAKE DESIGN
For the design shown opposite, you need a very tall cake so that you have a base on which to create a landscape. The cake was approximately 20 cm in diameter and 24 cm in depth. If you place the cake on a large board, you can place little characters all around the cake landscape. I have clouds and a sun in the sky, but you could add a little house, car or tree on the horizon.

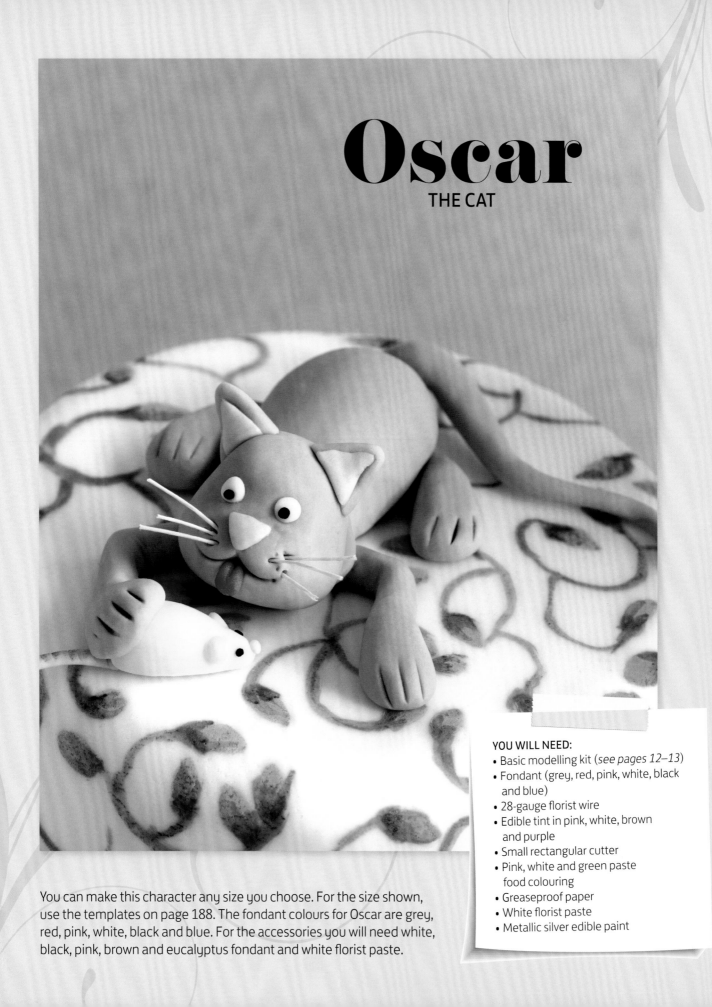

# Oscar
## THE CAT

You can make this character any size you choose. For the size shown, use the templates on page 188. The fondant colours for Oscar are grey, red, pink, white, black and blue. For the accessories you will need white, black, pink, brown and eucalyptus fondant and white florist paste.

**YOU WILL NEED:**
- Basic modelling kit (*see pages 12–13*)
- Fondant (grey, red, pink, white, black and blue)
- 28-gauge florist wire
- Edible tint in pink, white, brown and purple
- Small rectangular cutter
- Pink, white and green paste food colouring
- Greaseproof paper
- White florist paste
- Metallic silver edible paint

1

Roll 2 balls of light grey fondant for the body and the head.

2

Roll the larger ball into a cone shape, making sure it's quite thin at the smaller end.

3

Lay the cone on your work surface and flatten the smaller end with your thumb.

4

Roll the smaller ball into an egg shape.

5

Mark the position of the ears with a pin tool.

6

Gently draw the top of the mouth with a scalpel. Mark the eyes using a pin tool.

7

Use the pin tool to make a large hole in the centre of the mouth where the tongue will be inserted.

8

For the tongue, make a red cone, flatten, then cut off the point. Score a line down the middle.

9

Glue the tongue in place as shown.

10

For the nose, make a pink cone shape. Cut off and discard the rounded end.

11

Glue the nose in position as shown.

12

Make holes for whiskers using a pin tool.

13

Cut 6 strips of 28-gauge florist wire 2 cm long. (See Top Tip on page 168.)

14

Push the wire or noodles into the holes.

**15**

For the ears, roll 2 grey balls. Using your finger and thumb, pinch one end of each ball to make a cone.

**16**

Take 1 cone and flatten, then cut off and discard the rounded end. Cut out a pink triangle.

**17**

Glue the triangle into the ear, then repeat steps 16–17 to make the other ear.

**18**

Glue the ears into the slots made in step 5.

TOP TIP
As an edible alternative for whiskers, you could use rice noodles instead of florist wire.

**19**

Glue the head onto the flattened end of the body.

**20**

Cut a strip of light blue fondant to make a collar.

**21**

Apply glue behind the neck and secure the collar over the join. Remove any excess fondant.

**22**

To make the back legs, roll 2 balls of grey fondant into cones, making them slightly curved.

**23**

Take 1 leg and make 3 grooves in the wide end of the cone, to form a paw.

**24**

Repeat step 23 for the other leg, ensuring the paw faces the other way. Glue the legs in place.

**25**

To make the arms, roll 2 balls of fondant into long cone shapes as shown.

**26**

Take 1 arm and flatten the wider end of the cone, turning it slightly as you do so.

**27**

Bend the arm to create an elbow, then cut the fondant about 1 cm above the elbow.

**28**

Make 3 grooves in the paw. Repeat steps 26–8 for the other arm, making sure it faces the other way.

**29**

Glue the arms in place. While the fondant is still soft, make a ball shape in which to slot the mouse under one paw.

**30**

Slot the mouse into the cat's paw (see below for how to make the mouse).

**31**

For the tail, roll a long cone and bend the wider end as shown. Create a wave in the tail and flatten the wide end.

**32**

Glue the tail in place underneath the cat's bottom. Your finished cat should look like this.

### Milo the Mouse

**1**

Roll a ball of white fondant into a cone and gently pinch the pointed end.

**2**

For the ears, roll 2 tiny white balls and place them in the correct position as shown. Gently press and smooth them into place with a small ball tool.

**3**

Add 2 tiny black fondant balls for eyes and a pink ball for the nose. Dust around the ears and the sides of the body with light pink edible tint.

**4**

To make a tail, roll a thin cone of light pink fondant and mark lines along it with the back of a scalpel. Make as many mice as you wish.

**TOP TIP**
As an alternative to using tiny balls of fondant to make eyes, you could use non-pareils (also known as hundreds and thousands) in an appropriate colour.

### Floor boards

Cover a cake board in brown fondant, then, using a rectangle cutter, gently make a herringbone pattern all over the surface of the fondant.

Dust over the lines with brown edible tint, then darken the lines themselves with purple tint.

**TOP TIP**
Dark purple edible tint is perfect for dark shadows. You can use it for everything from lines in floors to shadows under eyes. Always use dark purple rather than black, as black tends to be too harsh.

### Wallpaper

Using paste food colouring and a size 2 brush, paint light pink petals on the surface of your cake.

Using a size 1 or 2 brush, paint darker lines around the base of each petal to make a 'V' shape.

Join the petals together using green paste food colouring mixed with water. If the green is too dark, add a little yellow paste food colouring.

### Skirting board and mouse door

Wrap eucalyptus-coloured fondant around the cake base. Make lines using a wheel tool and dust on light pink, brown and yellow edible tint.

Make a door template from greaseproof paper. Cut out a door using brown fondant. Make vertical lines using a wheel tool.

Glue the door in place and make some softer lines with the wheel tool to give the appearance of wood.

Glue 2 more strips of brown fondant around the door frame and add lines with the wheel tool.

Using florist paste, make a white door knob and 2 hinges, then paint them with light silver or gold metallic paint.

**CAKE DESIGN**
For the design opposite, I have made a cake that is 16 cm in diameter and 20 cm in depth. The cake sits on a large round board (33 cm in diameter) so that there is enough space for the mice to sit next to the cake. The floor is intentionally haphazard to give a rustic effect.

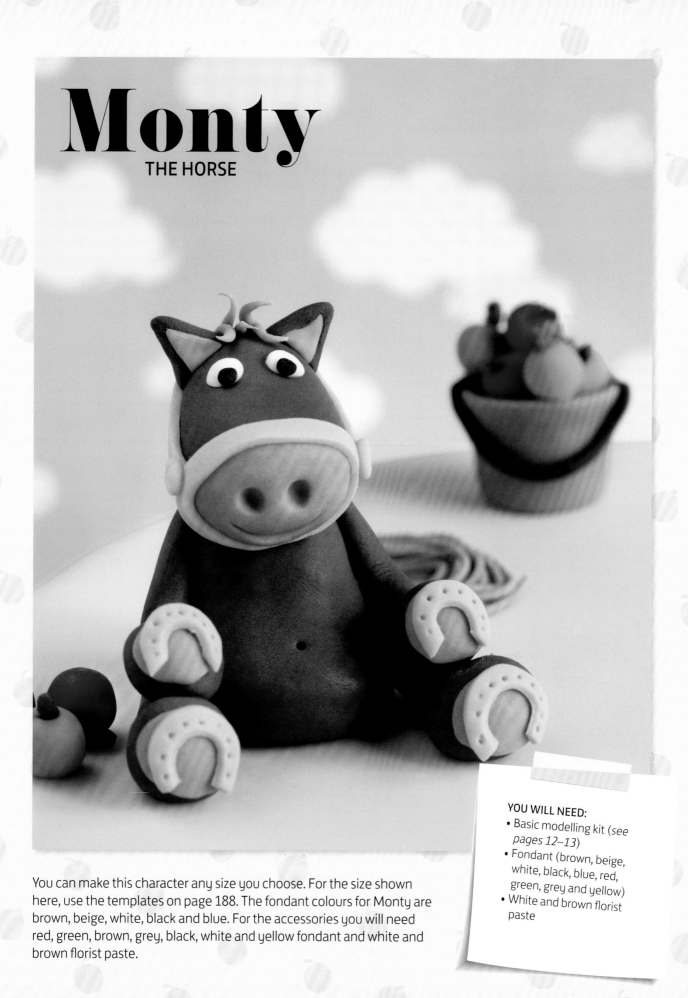

# Monty
## THE HORSE

You can make this character any size you choose. For the size shown here, use the templates on page 188. The fondant colours for Monty are brown, beige, white, black and blue. For the accessories you will need red, green, brown, grey, black, white and yellow fondant and white and brown florist paste.

**YOU WILL NEED:**
- Basic modelling kit (*see pages 12–13*)
- Fondant (brown, beige, white, black, blue, red, green, grey and yellow)
- White and brown florist paste

Roll 2 balls of brown fondant for the body and the head.

Roll the larger ball into a cone, making sure the bottom end is much bigger than the top.

Using your thumb, press down the front, in the middle, to make a fat tummy.

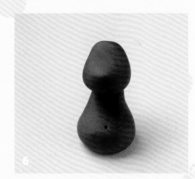

Insert a piece of spaghetti as shown, then make a belly button using a pin tool.

Roll the smaller ball into an egg shape.

TOP TIP
Cows and horses are made in very similar ways, the main difference being that the horse's head is longer and thinner than the cow's. A horse's head is similar in length to a dog's.

Position the head on the spaghetti to check that it's in proportion with the body.

Roll out some beige fondant and cut out an oval shape about the same size as the front of the face.

Glue the oval to the face as shown, then smooth out the edges.

Using a small ball tool, make 2 indents for the nostrils.

Use the wide end of a size 2 nozzle to make a smile.

Mark 2 holes for the eyes using a pin tool, then use the side of the pin tool to make grooves where the ears will sit.

Roll 2 balls of white fondant and glue them over the holes you made for the eyes.

Roll 2 small black fondant balls for the pupils and glue them in place.

To make the ears, roll 2 balls of brown fondant. Take 1 ball and pinch between your thumb and finger to make a triangle.

Squash the fondant flat and cut off the rounded end. Make a smaller beige triangle and glue this onto the centre of the brown triangle.

Repeat steps 14–15 to make the other ear (making sure they're the same size).

Glue the ears in place, in the grooves you made in step 11.

TOP TIP
The eyes will dictate the personality of your character. To make them look cute, point the eyes up to one side. For a cheeky or patronising look, angle them down to one side. For intelligence, point the eyes forward. For craziness, make them cross-eyed!

Cut 4 strips of blue fondant (this includes some spare ones, in case you break any).

Glue 1 strip of fondant over the seam around the nose.

Glue another strip around the back of the head, then join it to the first strip at the sides.

To cover the join, roll a small ball of blue fondant and glue it in place.

Using a scalpel, mark a cross on the blue ball.

To make the hair, roll some small pointed cones of beige fondant, then glue them in place between the ears.

TOP TIP
When working with brown fondant, I usually add a small amount of white. This is because pure brown tends to go very dark and makes it difficult to see the detail on the features.

To make the legs, roll 2 balls of brown fondant into cones.

Glue a circle of beige fondant onto the wide end of each cone.

To make the horseshoes, use a tear cutter to cut 2 blue fondant shapes.

Using a smaller tear cutter, cut a piece out of the centre of the 2 larger shapes.

Use a scalpel to cut off the pointed ends, to make 2 horseshoes.

Glue the horseshoes to the beige circles and mark little holes around the shoes with a pin tool.

Glue the legs in place on either side of the body. You could also glue the head in position at this point.

TOP TIP
Always plan the full design of your cake before you start. This way you will ensure all characters are looking in the correct direction and are in proportion with each other. As a rule of thumb, the average depth of a character on a cake is 8 cm and on a cupcake it is 5 cm.

To make the arms, roll 2 balls of brown fondant into a cone and bend each one in the middle to make a right angle.

Repeat steps 26–9 to make 2 more horseshoes.

Glue the arms in place so they are resting on the legs.

To make the hair, use a craft gun with a multi-strand hair nozzle.

Roll a sausage of beige fondant and insert into the craft gun. Screw on the nozzle lid.

TOP TIP
When using a craft gun with fondant, add extra white vegetable fat to the fondant before you put it in the gun. This is to prevent the gun from drying out the fondant as it squeezes it out.

Pump out the hair until it's the length you require. Use your fingers to break it from the gun and attach the strands at one end to make a tail.

Glue the tail to the back of the horse so that he's sitting on it. Your horse is now finished.

## Apples

Roll balls of red and green fondant and make a small indent in the top of each one using a ball tool. Roll some short cones of brown fondant and glue one in each indent.

## Bucket

Roll a ball of grey fondant into a cone. Cut off the top and bottom of the cone.

Using your thumb and finger, pinch around the edge of the wide surface to make a rim.

**TOP TIP**
Do as much modelling as you can using just your fingers; only use a tool when necessary to make the shape more accurate.

To make a handle, roll a strip of black florist paste and bend it into a curve. Allow it to dry for 10 minutes.

While the florist paste is drying, finish the bucket. Tap the top against your work surface to make it level.

Using a large ball tool, push the fondant against your finger to make a rim.

Attach the handle to the bucket, then add some of your apples (you may need to glue these in place).

## Fence

To make the fence, roll 2 long strips of white florist paste and 4 shorter strips with a point cut at the tip. Glue the long strips on top of the shorter strips.

To hold the strips together, glue 2 or 3 pieces of spaghetti to the back of the shorter strips of fondant.

Turn over the fence. Make little holes in the top of your cake in line with the spaghetti, to avoid breaking it when you push it into the cake. Glue the fence to the top of your cake.

CAKE DESIGN
In the picture opposite, I have set the horse beside a small barn on a large round cake (30 cm in diameter). The barn is made from 2 rectangular cakes, with the roof carved from cake. The cakes are covered in red and brown fondant.

## Barn

Cover your cake in red fondant and use a wheel tool to make wood markings (lots of small irregular lines will look very effective). Make a roof using brown fondant.

Add marks to the roof, as in step 1. Attach a door made from white strips, a star and a length of florist paste rolled up to look like rope. Glue the rope to a small knob of grey fondant and attach to the barn.

# Templates

If you wish to make your characters the same size as those shown in the book, you can use these templates as a guide.

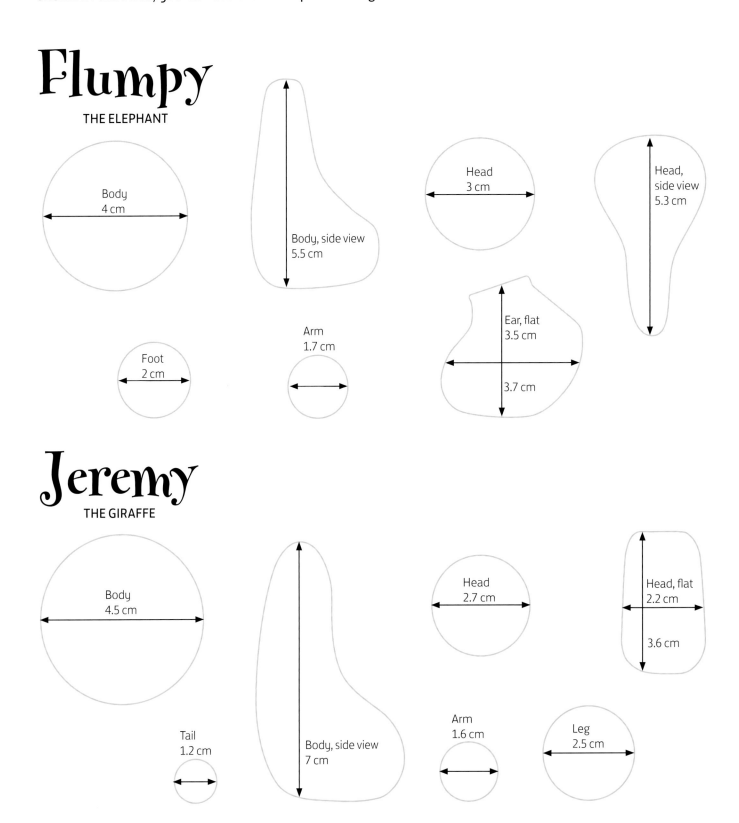

## Flumpy
### THE ELEPHANT

Body
4 cm

Body, side view
5.5 cm

Head
3 cm

Head, side view
5.3 cm

Foot
2 cm

Arm
1.7 cm

Ear, flat
3.5 cm

3.7 cm

## Jeremy
### THE GIRAFFE

Body
4.5 cm

Body, side view
7 cm

Head
2.7 cm

Head, flat
2.2 cm

3.6 cm

Tail
1.2 cm

Arm
1.6 cm

Leg
2.5 cm

# Maloo
## THE MONKEY

Body
4 cm

Body, side view
4.5 cm

Head, base
2.5 cm

Head, top
2 cm

Arm
1.7 cm

Leg
2.3 cm

Tail
2 cm

# Ariel
## THE LION

Body
4.3 cm

Body,
side view
5.7 cm

Head
3 cm

Head,
side view
3.4 cm

Arm
2 cm

Leg
2 cm

Tail
1.5 cm

# Zachery
## THE ZEBRA

Body
4.3 cm

Body, front view
4 cm

4 cm

Arm
1.5 cm

Leg
2 cm

Head
3 cm

Tail
2 cm

# Eden

**THE FAIRY**

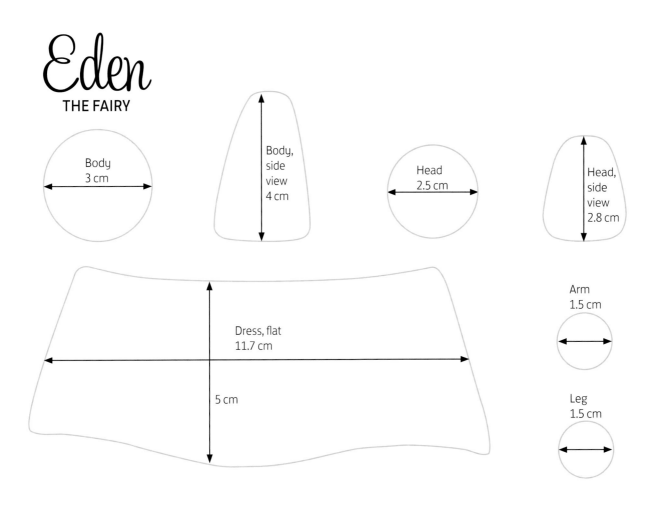

Body
3 cm

Body,
side
view
4 cm

Head
2.5 cm

Head,
side
view
2.8 cm

Arm
1.5 cm

Dress, flat
11.7 cm

5 cm

Leg
1.5 cm

# Darcie

**THE FAIRY**

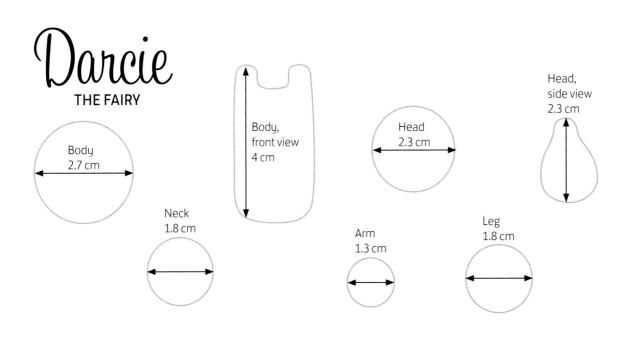

Body
2.7 cm

Neck
1.8 cm

Body,
front view
4 cm

Head
2.3 cm

Head,
side view
2.3 cm

Arm
1.3 cm

Leg
1.8 cm

# Matilda
**THE FAIRY**

Body
3 cm

Body, side view
2 cm

Head
2.5 cm

Leg
1.5 cm

Arm
1.2 cm

# Bramble & Ben
**THE FAIRIES**

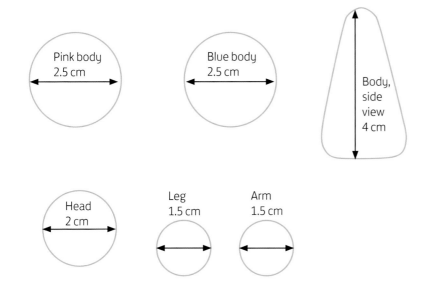

Pink body
2.5 cm

Blue body
2.5 cm

Body,
side
view
4 cm

Head
2 cm

Leg
1.5 cm

Arm
1.5 cm

# Gooba

## THE ALIEN

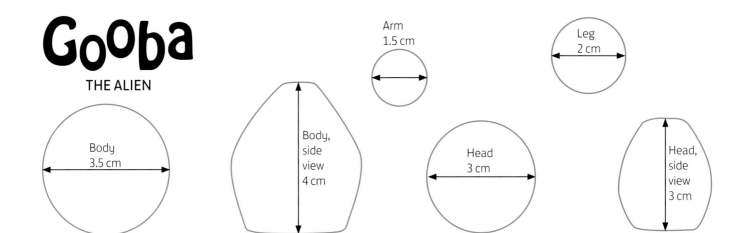

Body
3.5 cm

Body, side view
4 cm

Arm
1.5 cm

Leg
2 cm

Head
3 cm

Head, side view
3 cm

# Blinky

## THE ALIEN

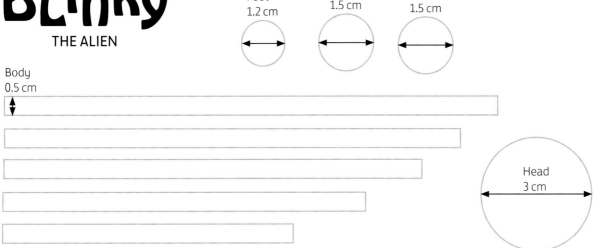

Foot
1.2 cm

Eye
1.5 cm

Arm
1.5 cm

Body
0.5 cm

Head
3 cm

# Boppa

## THE MONSTER

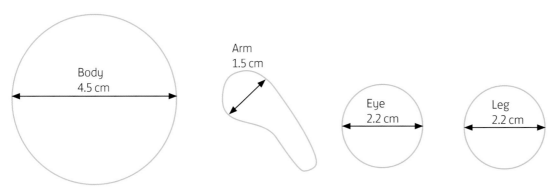

Body
4.5 cm

Arm
1.5 cm

Eye
2.2 cm

Leg
2.2 cm

# Bertie

**THE ALIEN**

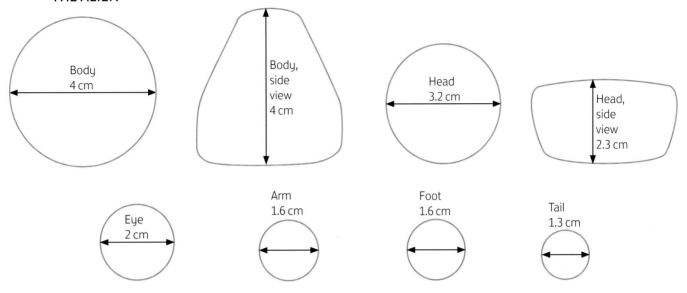

Body
4 cm

Body, side view 4 cm

Head
3.2 cm

Head, side view 2.3 cm

Eye
2 cm

Arm
1.6 cm

Foot
1.6 cm

Tail
1.3 cm

# Giggles

**THE MONSTER**

Body
4.5 cm

Body, side view 5 cm

Leg
1.5 cm

Arm
1.5 cm

# ROXY

## THE OCTOPUS

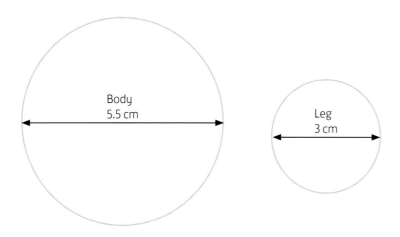

Body
5.5 cm

Leg
3 cm

Leg length 16 cm

# TONTO

## THE TURTLE

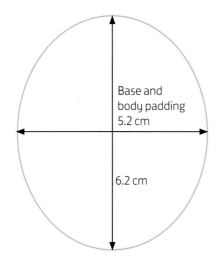

Base and body padding
5.2 cm

6.2 cm

Neck
2 cm

Head
3.5 cm

Head, side view
4.3 cm

Arm
1.8 cm

Leg
1.5 cm

# CHARLIE

## THE PARROT

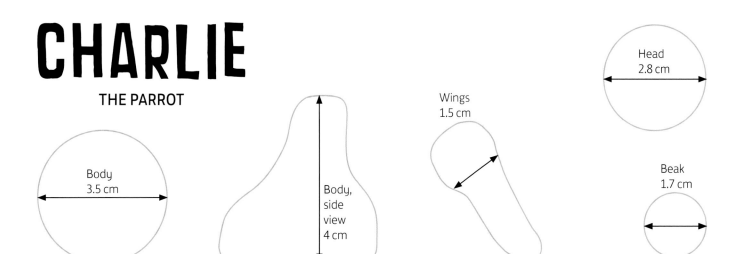

Body
3.5 cm

Body,
side
view
4 cm

Wings
1.5 cm

Head
2.8 cm

Beak
1.7 cm

# BOOMER

## THE FISH

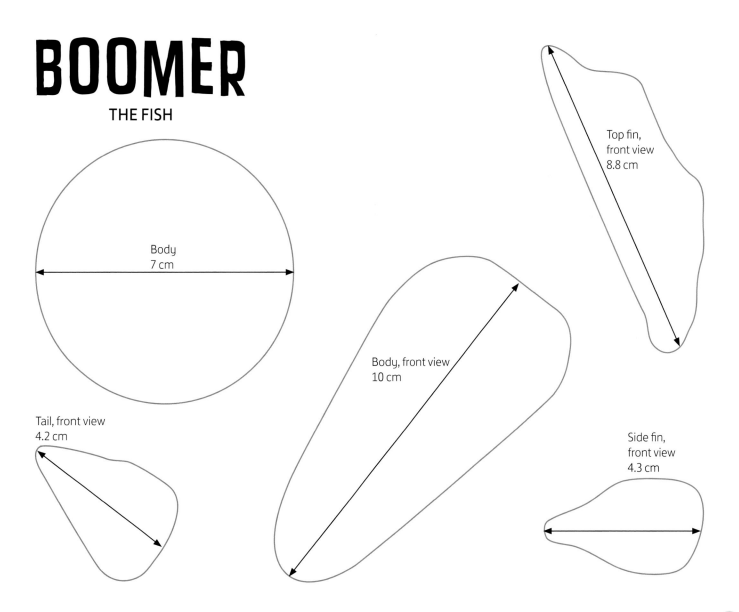

Body
7 cm

Top fin,
front view
8.8 cm

Tail, front view
4.2 cm

Body, front view
10 cm

Side fin,
front view
4.3 cm

# Monty
## THE HORSE

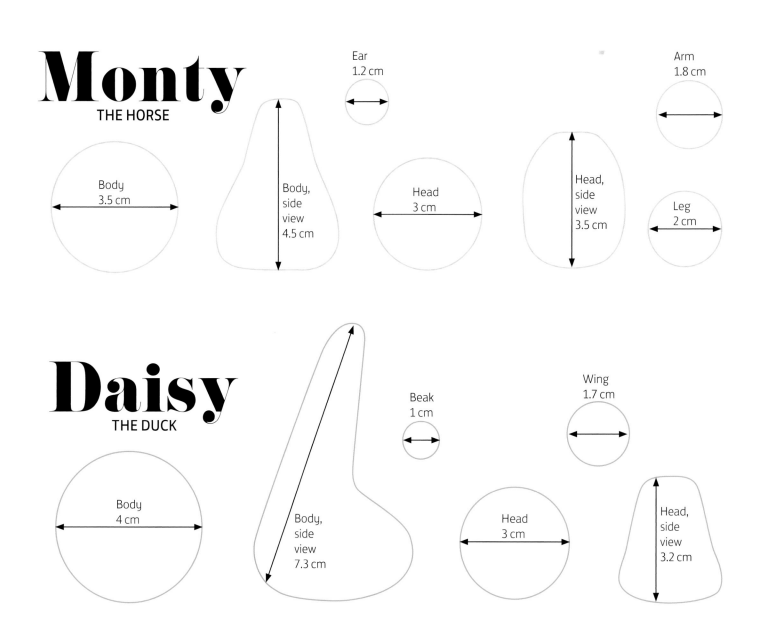

Ear
1.2 cm

Arm
1.8 cm

Body
3.5 cm

Body, side view
4.5 cm

Head
3 cm

Head, side view
3.5 cm

Leg
2 cm

# Daisy
## THE DUCK

Body
4 cm

Body, side view
7.3 cm

Beak
1 cm

Wing
1.7 cm

Head
3 cm

Head, side view
3.2 cm

# Oscar
## THE CAT

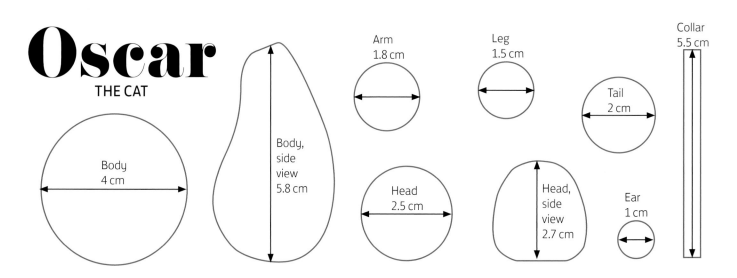

Arm
1.8 cm

Leg
1.5 cm

Collar
5.5 cm

Body
4 cm

Body, side view
5.8 cm

Tail
2 cm

Head
2.5 cm

Head, side view
2.7 cm

Ear
1 cm

# Barnaby
### THE SHEEP

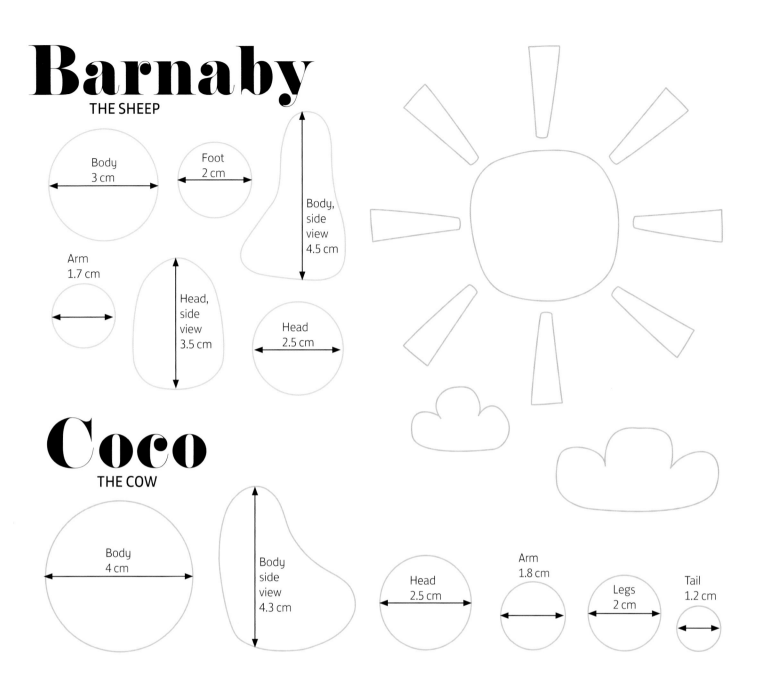

Body
3 cm

Foot
2 cm

Body,
side
view
4.5 cm

Arm
1.7 cm

Head,
side
view
3.5 cm

Head
2.5 cm

# Coco
### THE COW

Body
4 cm

Body
side
view
4.3 cm

Head
2.5 cm

Arm
1.8 cm

Legs
2 cm

Tail
1.2 cm

# Rosie
### THE PIG

Body
3.5 cm

Body,
side
view
4.2 cm

Head
2.5 cm

Leg
2 cm

Arm
2 cm

# SUPPLIERS

Everything used in this book is available from specialist cake decorating suppliers and, increasingly, in supermarkets. You can also purchase everything you need for cake decorating and modelling in the Pretty Witty Cakes online shop, which ships products all over the world. You can find us at **www.prettywittycakes.co.uk**.

We also teach online cake-decorating classes that are available 24 hours a day, 7 days a week, anywhere in the world. Suzi and her team of around 20 tutors present everything from basic baking to advanced cake making and decorating. There are members of the online tutorial site located all around the world in over 47 countries. To become a member of the online tutorial site, visit **www.prettywittycakes.co.uk**.

Throughout the year, we also host live classes and private one-to-one classes, and Suzi is a regular demonstrator and guest speaker at international cake shows.

# INDEX

To my husband and best friend James who has given me all the support I could ever wish for.

This book has been such fun to create and many memories will remain with me forever.

I would like to thank everyone who works at Pretty Witty Cakes, who have enabled me to spend time working on this book. In particular, I want to give special thanks to Amber, who makes my life so much easier every day in the kitchen and for her contribution to sections of this book. I also want to thank Kate, whose hard work and loyalty has enabled me to devote hundreds of hours to this book, knowing that my inbox was in safe hands.

I would also like to thank my publisher and the team at Quadrille: Alison Cathie, Jane O' Shea and Lisa Pendreigh.
A very special thanks to Nikki Ellis, who was with me from beginning to end of writing this book and whose enthusiasm was truly infectious. I also appreciated the fact that Nikki never failed to come to all our meetings armed with packets of biscuits and patiently assisted and provided invaluable advice on all those tiny details in the images.

A very big thank you goes to my fabulous photography team who were often working long into the night on our photo-shoots. I shall have memories of chewy fish sweets and the amazing Malou Burger forever. To be able to work with a team who make you laugh so much, especially on such long days, was an absolute privilege. Special thanks also goes to Sheila Udeagu who was a total joy to work with, as well as Polly Webb-Wilson and Tom and Ben.

I would also like to thank Katie Golsby for her guidance and expertise in editing the copy in the book and for patiently waiting for me to reply to her emails. Her advice on text layout was so helpful.

With so many teachers now teaching at Pretty Witty Cakes, I have been privileged to be able to talk about my ideas with some amazing cake makers and learn from many others. I would like to

make special thanks to my good friend Kaysie Lackey, who first introduced me to colour shapers in 2011. I would also like to thank the lovely Rachel Hill, who is not only a great cake maker but a friend and someone who has given me guidance and advice during 2013. Thank you May Clee Cadman for your pearls of wisdom about writing cake books.

I would also like to take a special opportunity to thank Hannah, who helps me juggle motherhood with business, letting me know that at times when I was working my children were well cared for and happy.

Most of all, a heartfelt thank you to all our customers who have supported us both past and present. I met so many of you in 2010 when I started the business, and so many of you remain loyal customers to this day – and, for that, I thank you from the bottom of my heart.

I would also like to thank several of my amazing suppliers, who have delivered things to me at short notice and often offered me sound business advice. Particular mention goes to Mike and Karen of FPC Sugarcraft.

A very special thank you goes to some of my lifelong friends, who watched me start Pretty Witty Cakes from scratch and have given me the strength and support that only friends can give. Special thanks in particular goes to Dave Hall – one of the most talented artists I have ever met and the only person who can take my words and turn them into an exact picture of what is in my head. Special thanks also goes to Phillip Hall who, from the other side of the world has offered sound business and personal advice to me from the day I started Pretty Witty Cakes.

Finally, I would like to thank my husband James and my two children Barnaby and Bertie. I am so privileged to have them as my family and, although my family is small, it is the best little family in the world. I could not wish for a better and more supportive husband and two more beautiful and loving children. Every character and cake I make starts and ends with you.

---

PUBLISHING DIRECTOR Jane O'Shea
COMMISSIONING EDITOR Lisa Pendreigh
PROJECT EDITOR Katie Golsby
CREATIVE DIRECTOR Helen Lewis
SENIOR DESIGNER Nicola Ellis
DESIGN ASSISTANT Emily Lapworth
PHOTOGRAPHER Malou Burger
STYLIST Polly Webb-Wilson
PRODUCTION DIRECTOR Vincent Smith
PRODUCTION CONTROLLER Sarah Neesam

First published in 2014 by
Quadrille Publishing Ltd
Alhambra House
27–31 Charing Cross Road
London WC2H 0LS
www.quadrille.co.uk

Text and character design © 2014 Suzi Witt
Photography © 2014 Malou Burger
Design and layout © 2014 Quadrille Publishing Ltd

British Library Cataloguing-in-Publication Data:
A catalogue record for this book is available from the British Library.

ISBN 978 1 84949 328 4

Printed in China.